Bethany Sund[...]

MW00943766

ON-THE-GO
DEVOTIONAL

200 DEVOTIONS FOR TEENS

WRITTEN BY LESLIE HUDSON

PUBLISHING GROUP
Nashville, Tennessee

978-1-5359-7255-0

Published by B&H Publishing Group
Nashville, Tennessee

Dewey Decimal Classification: 242.63
Subject Heading: DEVOTIONAL LITERATURE / TEENAGERS / YOUTH

1 2 3 4 5 6 • 23 22 21 20 19

INTRODUCTION

Let's face it. The world is crazy. With all the buzzing about this way and that, it's a little daunting to sit down and have any amount of quiet time. It feels like it's just another thing we have to squeeze into the day. We get it. Trying to keep good grades, make certain teams, and participate in clubs is hectic enough!

How can anyone be expected to read the Bible for hours on end when the world is spinning out of control? That's why this devotional exits. Each page is packed with strong messages about a God who loves you and wants you to know that with Him, you'll make it through the day. Whether you read it in your room, on the bus, or at the lunch table, our hope is that you take these messages wherever you are, even on the go.

The LORD is my shepherd; I have what I need.
(Psalm 23:1)

There's a good chance you've heard this verse in church, at funerals, or maybe in a prayer. The words might seem familiar, but consider the truths contained in this short statement:

- The author (David) knew all about sheep; he was a shepherd for years. He knew sheep were helpless, defenseless, and tended to panic.
- Sheep are only safe when they have a shepherd who guides them to good food and fresh water while also keeping them away from predators and other dangers.
- Any sheep that breaks away from the herd is immediately at risk.

David killed a lion and a bear, as well as the giant Goliath, all before adulthood. He led God's people into battles and became their king. He probably seemed invincible at times.

But even with all these skills, he was still humble enough to realize his relationship to God: sheep to shepherd. *Because* God was his shepherd, David was confident he was protected, fed, and loved.

TO GO . . .

Also read Psalm 23:2–6 and John 10:11–18. As you go, ponder: What does a life look like when God is the true shepherd?

And Mary said: "My soul praises the greatness of the Lord, and my spirit rejoices in God my Savior, because he has looked with favor on the humble condition of his servant." (Luke 1:46–48)

Yesterday, we looked at David's willingness to be humble; today we see the words of another famous Bible character: Mary, the mother of Jesus.

Like David, Mary had many reasons to feel honored: an angel had just visited her and told her she had found favor with God, that God was with her, and that she would be the mother of the Messiah. Instead of considering her own worthiness, however, she chose to focus on God.

- Maybe you're like Mary, a little afraid of the future and what God has planned for you.
- Maybe you know God has called you to something but don't know exactly what that is.
- Maybe you hear God speaking to you but don't know why.

Take a lesson from Mary: tell God you are His servant and that you're willing to obey. Praise Him for His greatness but also for choosing you to be His servant.

TO GO . . .

Also read 1 Samuel 2:1. As you go, rejoice that God uses you in His plans.

Do nothing out of selfish ambition or conceit, but in humility consider others as more important than yourselves. (Philippians 2:3)

Selfishness is something we can quickly identify in others, but we're usually not so great at seeing it in ourselves.

There is no room for selfishness in God's kingdom. He is God; He is the only One who is all-knowing, all-powerful, and has a perfect plan.

Selfishness creeps into our lives when we attempt to put ourselves at the center of our lives instead of God (who, by the way, deserves it). Each of us is selfish in some area:

- with our time
- with our priorities
- with our relationships
- with our focus

Basically, we don't like people—or even God—telling us what to do, but that's not humility. Humility is admitting that God is who He says He is and allowing Him to have the position He deserves: Lord and King.

How do we know we're living selfishly? We still put ourselves first. Start humbling yourself by considering others first, and you'll start giving God first place in your heart and mind.

TO GO . . .

Read Philippians 2:1–11. As you go, invite God to show you the areas where you're selfish.

Humble yourselves before the Lord, and he will exalt you. (James 4:10)

Humbling yourself is not the same thing as putting yourself down. We've all met people who can't take a compliment: "I like your shirt." "Oh, it's old and ugly." That's not humility; that's self-hate. God doesn't desire for us to belittle ourselves. He does, however, expect us to humble ourselves.

Biblical humility is recognizing where you rank in the universe: way, way, way below God. You know who else is there with you? Everyone classified as human.

Consider these statements of humility:

- I make mistakes.
- I am not perfect and won't be.
- God, however, is perfect and still chose me to be His child.

The same statements could be said about your best friend, your pastor, even the most vile and hateful person you know. Humility comes only when we let go of ourselves and hold onto Almighty God.

Once you accept these statements about yourself and others, you're on the path to true humility.

TO GO . . .

Read the context of this verse in James 4:1–12. As you go, say the three statements of humility about yourself and someone else.

> *For the LORD takes pleasure in his people; he adorns the humble with salvation. (Psalm 149:4)*

You may not use the word *adorn* often. Whenever you make something more visually attractive, you've adorned it. Maybe that means hanging up some posters, nailing some barnwood, detailing your car, or sprinkling some glitter. You've seen it on DIY websites or home improvement shows.

Adorning something shows your pride and love for that thing. We don't adorn things that mean nothing to us; we adorn the things that are precious: our rooms, Christmas trees, or even the spot in the basement where we watch television or read. We want to bring our personal touch of affection to those special things.

God does the same with us! His people please Him with their faith, and He adorns us with salvation.

Never thought about it before? Consider this—those who know and follow Jesus . . .

- look more like Jesus.
- know and believe His Word.
- are given every spiritual blessing.

You, child of God, bring Him pleasure.

TO GO . . .

Consider how Psalm 51:17 sheds light on this idea. As you go, thank God for adorning you with salvation. Ask Him to reveal what that means.

I will look favorably on this kind of person: one who is humble, submissive in spirit, and trembles at my word. (Isaiah 66:2)

Many people make daily checklists for themselves: Clean room? *Check.* Homework? *Check.* Chores done? *Check.*

Others make checklists for their futures: Graduate high school? *Check.* Get into college? *Check.* Good job? *Check.*

God's checklists don't often look like our checklists. Did you catch the one He made in Isaiah 66? God's favorite people . . .

- are humble.
- have submissive spirits.
- tremble at His Word.

There's a good chance you don't put those on your daily or long-term checklists, but maybe you should. Being humble and submitting to God isn't something that comes naturally; we must choose to place ourselves in His control, yield our plans to His and trust Him with the results.

Many people—even Christians—can't handle giving up control of their lives; they don't want God dictating their checklists.

But when we know Him as He describes Himself in His Word—when it makes us tremble—our faith is strengthened so that we can.

TO GO . . .

Discover all the ways God describes Himself in Isaiah 66. As you go, consider one area of your life that you keep from God's authority.

> *"Take up my yoke and learn from me, because I am lowly and humble in heart, and you will find rest for your souls." (Matthew 11:29)*

Oxen are some of the most powerful animals used in farming. (You've heard the phrase, "strong as an ox." Well, there's a reason for it!) But since they typically weigh 1000 pounds or more, they need to learn how to be an ox that does its job well or they are totally out of control.

So one ox is yoked to another: the younger learns from the older, they are able to harness their strength together, and the younger sees what ox life actually looks like.

We are invited to be yoked to Jesus. Since He never commands us to do something without equipping us, his invitation also includes learning from Him.

Reflect on how Jesus describes Himself:

- He is lowly.
- He is humble.
- He knows where to find rest.

When we walk with Jesus, we understand the value of true humility and complete rest.

TO GO . . .

Discover what Paul says about a yoke in Galatians 5:1. As you go, picture yourself with a wooden yoke, connecting you to Jesus.

"Therefore, whoever humbles himself like this child—this one is the greatest in the kingdom of heaven." (Matthew 18:4)

When you think back on your childhood, you likely remember the lack of freedom:

- You ate what someone else made for you.
- You went wherever your parents took you.
- You went to bed whenever they told you.

Hopefully you have many wonderful memories from your childhood, but the freedoms of getting older are also pretty great. Likely, you hear everyone telling you that it's time to start acting your age (or older) and growing up in many ways.

Except one.

Jesus told His disciples that they needed to humble themselves, like a child. What does that even mean?

Well, look at the list above. When someone chose your meals or outings or bedtime, did you think, *I could have done this better*? No! You accepted your role as child and their role as adult.

Christians are to take the same approach to life: we are the creation, He is God. We trust His path, His plan, and His purposes for us.

TO GO . . .

Read Matthew 18:1–9 to see the whole scene. As you go, speak aloud to Jesus: "I trust you to lead me."

9 HUMILITY

Humility, the fear of the LORD, results in wealth, honor, and life. (Proverbs 22:4)

Wealth and honor sound like pretty good things, right? Money to spare, combined with the respect of people around you, equals a desirable life.

But this isn't wealth and honor like the world gives.

This is God's wealth and honor. You see, wealth and honor from the world makes us vain, self-absorbed, and dismissive of God.

God's version of wealth and honor comes only *after* we are humble because of our confidence that God is who He says He is. When wealth and honor are our goal, they ruin our faith and relationship with the Lord. But when knowing God and making Him great is our goal, He gives us wealth and honor that blesses us.

God's wealth and honor . . .

- help us trust Him.
- let us see ourselves honestly.
- bless others.
- glorify God.

God's version of wealth and honor might seem backward, but it is far more valuable and precious than anything the world has to offer.

TO GO . . .

See if you can find this same idea in Proverbs 3:16, 8:18, and 11:16. As you go, talk with someone you know who is honored by God.

Mankind, he has told each of you what is good and what it is the Lᴏʀᴅ requires of you: to act justly, to love faithfulness, and to walk humbly with your God. (Micah 6:8)

"I don't know God's will for my life."

"I wish God would show me what to do."

"I want to follow God, but I don't know where He's leading."

Maybe you've heard people say something similar. (Maybe you've said something similar.) But you never need to wonder what God's plan is for your life:

- Do justice.
- Love kindness.
- Walk humbly with God.

The three standards of Micah 6:8 encompass the three areas in which we choose to obey God:

- the needy ("do justice")
- people in your everyday life ("love kindness")
- your relationship with God ("walk humbly")

These are the basics of God's will for your life. You see, if you choose to do these things, everything else will fall into place. God will open the doors and point to the paths for you. Do your part; He'll do His.

TO GO . . .

Consider how Daniel 4:37 relates to today's verse. As you go, write down one specific way you will follow these standards today.

> *"For God loved the world in this way: He gave his one and only Son, so that everyone who believes in him will not perish but have eternal life." (John 3:16)*

Sometimes Scripture comes alive when we assign a mental image to a verse.

Think about John 3:16 for a moment. Even though you've probably heard it many times, what image comes to mind? Many people think of God loving the earth, as if Almighty God is looking down from heaven, giving a grandfatherly smile toward the ball of land and sea we call earth.

Maybe a better image would be this: God's love came through Jesus. Through His love, Jesus was able to walk up to each person on earth, offering a hug.

Even though God's love is for the entire world, His offer goes out to each and every one of us. We all have the opportunity to accept His love.

Some people take God's hug through Jesus. Some people don't. But everyone is offered it.

Have you accepted the love of God? It begins with believing Jesus is who the Bible says He is.

TO GO . . .

Read John 3:17–21 to understand the rest of Jesus' explanation. As you go, consider how you might put this image into someone's mind or heart today.

But God proves his own love for us in that while we were still sinners, Christ died for us. (Romans 5:8)

You've had to prove things for a while now:

- You proved your identity with your birth certificate.
- You proved you were healthy enough for sports with a physical.
- You proved you understood Algebra by passing that final.

You could prove your love for a certain band by singing along with every song. You could prove your love for your best friend by telling story after story after story of your adventures with them.

God has already proven His love for us: Christ died for us while we were still sinners.

It's ridiculous, really. Jesus chose to leave all the glories and perfection of heaven to come live and die—horribly—before a single person ever accepted Him as Savior. Let's personalize this: before you even thought about whether or not He was worthy of your faith, He had already died for you.

Like showing your mom that "A" in Algebra, proving your hard work, God has been standing there with His proof of love for you.

TO GO . . .

Look at what else God proves in 2 Samuel 22:26–27. As you go, consider how we can prove our love for God in response to His love for us.

> *The LORD your God is among you, a warrior who saves. He will rejoice over you with gladness. He will be quiet in his love. He will delight in you with singing. (Zephaniah 3:17)*

You're complex. Some people may see you as only one identity (studious, athletic, creative, talkative), but there's so much more to you. The people who know you best could give ten words to describe you.

It's painful when someone can't see past one identity. We all wish to get to know ourselves enough that others see all of our interesting, wonderful, and deep characteristics?

Sometimes people see God one-dimensionally: Judge. Creator. Miracle-worker.

How do you describe God? Is He powerful? Loving? Beautiful? Brave? Musical? Creative? Bold? Yes. He's all these things plus dozens of others.

Just like there is more to you than one description, there are many aspects of God. Look at the descriptions in Zephaniah 3:17:

- warrior
- rejoicer
- glad
- quiet in love
- delighted
- singer

Dare yourself to know God fully!

TO GO . . .

Get in the habit of circling every single description of God in Scripture. As you go, praise God for being so complex. Ask for ways to know Him better.

*See what great love the Father has given us that
we should be called God's children—and we are!
(1 John 3:1)*

Seeing is believing. Often, when we're trying unsuccessfully to describe something to a friend, we finally just say, "Come and see!"

The same holds true for God's love! In today's verse, John is inviting Christians to "see what great love the Father has given us." Maybe you've felt love, given love, or experienced love; but can we really see love? Yes!

God's love can be seen when . . .

- we receive undeserved kindness.
- we are loved and accepted by others.
- we sacrifice our time and energy to bless others.
- we choose to love, forgive, and help someone for no reason.

God's love is visible among His children. Just as people in the same family often look like each another, we look like God when we love others as He loves us. His love is visible in us for the whole world to see.

TO GO . . .

Read 1 John 3:1–3 to discover some of the ways we make God visible. As you go, ask God to give you the opportunity to make His love visible to others today.

But you, Lord, are a compassionate and gracious God, slow to anger and abounding in faithful love and truth. (Psalm 86:15)

Many of the psalms were intended to be sung. Psalm 86 is one of them. It was written by King David when he was obviously going through a difficult time. In it, he says:

- "I am poor and needy."
- "I call on you in the day of my distress."
- "Arrogant people have attacked me."
- "A gang of ruthless men intends to kill me."

We've all had the kinds of days when it seems like everything is against us. With all of our struggles, it's easy to feel overwhelmed.

But we would be wise to follow David's example: in the prayer of Psalm 86, he says "you" or "your" thirty-four times! Even though he is struggling, he chooses to focus on God. He sees that God is gracious, compassionate, and abounding in faithful love.

We can do the same. Choose to focus intently on God's qualities in the hardest times.

TO GO . . .

See if you can find every "you" and "your" in Psalm 86. As you go, consider how you've experienced God's faithful love. Say it out loud!

God's love has been poured out in our hearts
through the Holy Spirit who was given to us.
(Romans 5:5)

Children love to pour milk into their cereal or juice into a cup. But almost every kid has made the mistake of pouring too much and seeing the liquid overflow the container and making a mess.

Are you good at pouring? There's actually a skill to it: not too much, not too little. You get better at it as you get older.

Know who's great at pouring? God. Look at Romans 5:5. He has poured His love into our hearts! That may sound a little strange, but when we believe in Jesus for salvation, the Holy Spirit enables us to receive God's love. And God, who is an expert at pouring, is careful to place His love in our hearts with precision and care.

So what do we do with God's love in our hearts? Pour it out! We do so when we . . .

- share
- forgive
- bless
- encourage
- smile

We can be sure we have plenty of love to give!

TO GO . . .

Read about a woman who poured out her love for Jesus in Matthew 26:6–13. As you go, look for an opportunity to pour out God's love intentionally.

And we have come to know and to believe the love that God has for us. God is love, and the one who remains in love remains in God, and God remains in him. (1 John 4:16)

You've heard people tell you that God loves you. You've read it in the Bible. You've heard teachers and preachers say it.

But hearing about God's love is not the same as knowing it and believing it. You can hear all kinds of things, but you don't know or believe them unless your heart and mind are changed by it.

You know and believe God's love if:

- You can explain it to others.
- You remind yourself of it in every situation.
- It changes your attitude.
- It helps you make decisions.
- It becomes your identity.

Feel like you don't believe? Practice by saying, "Because God loves me, I will. . ."

Keeping God's love in our minds helps it remain in our hearts. When our hearts and minds are focused on the love of God, we remain in His love.

TO GO . . .

Read more about God's love in 1 John 4:17–21. As you go, sing, "Jesus Loves Me" aloud or silently.

I pray that you . . . may be able to comprehend with all the saints what is the length and width, height and depth of God's love, . . . so that you may be filled with all the fullness of God. (Ephesians 3:17–19)

Have you ever visited a place that took your breath away? Consider the mountains, the oceans, the Grand Canyon, or something similar.

Even if you saw photos or talked to people who had seen it, witnessing it for yourself was beyond comparison; no photo or description can ever truly grasp the real thing.

God's love is the same: It's so much more than you could ever describe or imagine.

And no matter how much you hear about it or see it in the lives of others, you simply cannot fathom the love of God until you experience it for yourself.

What do we know about God's love?

- Other believers know it.
- We find it in Christ.
- It surpasses knowledge.
- It fills us with God.

TO GO . . .

Read Paul's full blessing in Ephesians 3:14–21. As you go, ask God to help you realize the bigness of His love today.

19 GOD'S LOVE FOR US

Give thanks to the LORD, for he is good. His faithful love endures forever. (Psalm 136:1)

Everything you know of God comes from His love. We can't separate God's love from anything else about Him.

Because He is love:

- He blesses us.
- He invites us to know Him.
- He chooses to abide with us.
- His judgments are fair.
- His plan for us is perfect.

In Psalm 136, the phrase "His faithful love endures forever" is repeated in every single verse. You could read the entire psalm, skipping "His faithful love endures forever," and it would make perfect sense.

But that's not what the psalmist intended. He couldn't get more than a handful of words out of his mouth without being reminded of God's faithful love. When talking about God as Almighty, as Creator, as Supreme Ruler, or as Mighty Warrior, the refrain repeats, "His faithful love endures forever."

Let this psalm inspire you to focus on God's faithful love in every circumstance, great or small.

TO GO . . .

Read Psalm 136 and see for yourself! As you go, reflect on God's presence in your life. Rejoice in His faithful love!

*For as high as the heavens are above the earth,
so great is his faithful love toward those who fear
him. (Psalm 103:11)*

Love and fear don't often go together. It's rare that we love something
that causes us to fear.

Let's change the definition of *fear*: instead of meaning "afraid of," consider it to mean, "respect of power and authority." Hopefully you're not
afraid of your parents, but you respect their power and authority. That's
healthy fear. The same goes for sharks, high-voltage electricity, rock
climbing, or anything else that deserves our respect.

- When you *respectfully* fear your parents, you obey their rules.
- When you *respectfully* fear sharks, you swim in the ocean with
  caution.
- When you *respectfully* fear electricity, you keep metal away from
  outlets.
- When you *respectfully* fear rock climbing, you'll follow all safety
  guidelines.

Fearing God results in something unexpected; we catch a glimpse of
the immensity of His love. Our ability to comprehend God's humongous
love expands as we respectfully fear Him.

TO GO . . .

Read all of Psalm 103 and ask God to help you respectfully fear Him. As you go, consider how the love of God
and the fear of God work together.

"We love because he first loved us." (1 John 4:19)

How many times have you asked, "But why?" You've probably asked it of your parents when they gave you a curfew. You've probably asked it of your teacher when she assigned a paper.

Have you ever asked God "but why?"

- *But why should I read the Bible?*
- *But why can't I see You?*
- *But why is life so hard?*

No matter how old we get or how well we know the Bible, we never stop asking "Why?"; often, those things make us ask "why?" even more. Of all the commands in the Bible, the hardest one to obey is God's instruction to love others. (We ask, "Even mean people? Even the ones who hate us? Even the truly terrible?") The Bible says, yes!

But why? Because He loved us first. Before we were born, before we called out for salvation, before we believed, even before we took one obedient step, He loved us. And He still loves you when you're grumpy, when you're mean, and when you don't deserve it.

TO GO . . .

Read more about asking "Why?" in Psalm 10. As you go, choose to love a difficult person because God loved you first.

"The one who has my commands and keeps them is the one who loves me." (John 14:21)

"I love my puppy." "I love pizza." "I love that band." "I love to sleep."

We say we *love* many things. We even say we love God. But how do we know that our love is real?

Not to worry; Jesus Himself explained it in John 14:21: whoever has His commands and obeys them is the one who loves Him.

Let's break that down:

- "Has my commands" means we know what He says in the Bible and choose to remember it, think about it, and apply it.
- "Keeps them" means we choose to be changed by His Word, want to live by His instructions and believe His path is best.

So, according to Jesus, loving Him is more than just a feeling. (So much more!) It's a complete change of lifestyle. When we say we love Jesus, we choose to make His Word the foundation of all we believe, the way we live, and the decisions we make.

TO GO . . .

Read the context of this instruction in John 14:15–20. As you go, take a few minutes to consider if you obey Jesus out of love.

23 *HOW WE LOVE GOD*

*"Love the Lord your God with all your heart,
with all your soul, and with all your strength."
(Deuteronomy 6:5)*

Love is a crazy thing: it's one of the most powerful forces in the universe, and yet it never runs out. In fact, the more we love, the more love we have to give.

God is total love; He gets to set the rules for loving. Because He is Almighty Creator, He gets to tell us specifically how to love Him: with all our heart, all our soul, and all our strength.

What does that even mean? Well, the ancient words for *heart* and *soul* encompass everything that makes up who we are: our minds, our passions, our emotions, and our personalities. Add our "strength" to that, and we understand this verse means that we powerfully love God with everything that makes us who we are.

In order to follow this standard, we choose to love God . . .

- even when we're mad.
- even when we're overwhelmed.
- even when we don't want to.
- even when it's hard.

TO GO . . .

Read this instruction in Deuteronomy 6:4–9. As you go, consider some situations where you let emotions guide you instead of your love for God.

Above all, put on love, which is the perfect bond of unity. (Colossians 3:14)

When you got out of bed this morning, your clothes didn't magically appear on your body. They didn't leap from your closet or walk out of your dresser. You also didn't call your shoes to come put themselves on your feet.

No, you put them on, intentionally, with purpose.

Just as you wouldn't expect your clothing to put itself on, we shouldn't expect love to just appear in our hearts, either. We choose to put on love: intentionally and with purpose.

Putting on love takes a little forethought. Just like it's wise to know the forecast for the day before choosing which clothes and shoes to wear, we are wise to consider the kind of love we're going to need:

- "My teacher is grumpy today; she could use a smile."
- "My mom seems sad. I bet she needs some help."
- "That kid is always alone. I bet I can be his friend."

Putting on love is the perfect way to start your day.

TO GO . . .

Read about the concept of putting on Christ in Romans 13:11–14. As you go, picture yourself putting on love in each conversation today.

> *"If you keep my commands you will remain in my love, just as I have kept my Father's commands and remain in his love." (John 15:10)*

Let's be honest here: sometimes loving others just doesn't seem worth it.

- Sometimes you love people who don't love you back.
- Sometimes you love people who use it to hurt you.
- Sometimes the people you love die, move, or even choose not to be your friend, which hurts the worst.

Loving humans means taking huge risks. But loving Jesus comes with a promise: if we keep His commands, we remain in His love. That brings a holy joy that completes us! Here's how:

- Choose to believe the Bible is God's love story for us.
- Let His Word direct your life.

An obedient lifestyle is the key to remaining in the love of Jesus and experiencing complete joy!

TO GO . . .

Keep reading about love and joy working together in Galatians 5:22 and Philemon 7. As you go, take the step of faith to believe that Jesus' love will fill you with joy.

Love one another deeply as brothers and sisters.
Outdo one another in showing honor. (Romans
12:10)

Almost everyone is competitive in at least a few areas. You may compete in sports or some creative endeavor. You may race to get your homework finished, try to look better in a certain way, or make more money.

Sometimes competition can be a good thing. It gives us focus, builds determination, and provides an outlet. Other times, competition can reveal a side of us that is unkind, selfish, and wrongly motivated.

Do you dare accept a new competition, one that not only fuels your faith but also strengthens those around you? Try this one: "Outdo one another in showing honor."

What does it mean to show honor?

- We see the value in others: created by God and loved by Him.
- We choose to treat people with the value they deserve.

When we honor someone, we choose to speak encouragement, show kindness, and offer friendship.

Take the dare! Outdo others in showing honor.

TO GO . . .

The Greek word for *honor* is also found in 1 Corinthians 6:20; see if you can find it! As you go, choose one person you rarely honor and speak a good word about him or her today.

Dear friends, let us love one another, because love is from God, and everyone who loves has been born of God and knows God. (1 John 4:7)

Picture yourself sitting in a dark room. There are other people there, but you're all struggling because, well, darkness makes moving and communication difficult. Suddenly, someone turns on a light. It's just one bulb in the middle of the room, but that's all you needed. Now, you can see everyone clearly.

This is exactly what the love of God does.

We struggle with relationships among our family, friends, and acquaintances. We're not sure how to handle everyone's personalities and issues and faults, but God's love changes everything.

Like a light in darkness, God's love enters our lives, and He enables us to see one another clearly. We can choose to love because love has made everything different for us. Because God's love has entered every part of our lives, we treat everyone with love.

All who know God can love like this!

TO GO . . .

Find the words *light* and *love* in 1 John 2:10. How does that apply to 1 John 4:7? As you go, remember this verse each time you flip a light switch today.

A friend loves at all times, and a brother is born for a difficult time. (Proverbs 17:17)

Some people have many people they call "friends." Others have a handful in their lives who hold that title. Your definition of *friend* may be different from how someone else defines it, but each of us knows the difference between a friend and a stranger.

How does God identify a friend? Proverbs 17:17 reveals it: "A friend loves at all times." Let's put that into real-life terms:

- A friend loves you even when you're moody.
- A friend loves you even when you're unreasonable.
- A friend loves you even when you're struggling physically, spiritually, or emotionally.
- A friend sees your pain and your joy and walks with you in them.

When you look at it like that, there are very few people who meet God's definition of friend.

But don't use this as a measuring stick for others; use it on yourself. How do *you* measure up? Are you the type of friend defined in Proverbs 17:17? Can you honestly say you love at all times?

TO GO . . .

Find one way 2 Samuel 1:26 reflects this verse. As you go, ask God to show you how you can be a better friend today.

> *Show faithful love and compassion to one another.*
> *(Zechariah 7:9)*

These words from the prophet Zechariah actually came directly from God and went to the Israelites. This wasn't just a command in certain situations or with certain people; this was an ongoing, every-day and every-minute standard to show faithful love and compassion.

Faithful love and compassion reveal a genuine desire to show kindness. Faithful love chooses to hang on through difficult times; compassion sees the hurt of others and chooses to help bear the pain.

Some, however, aren't willing to love others like this; they'd rather not sacrifice their own time and effort. But according to God's standards, this command is non-negotiable; how we treat others reveals whether or not His love has truly saturated our hearts.

God Himself is the One who showed faithful love and compassion to us. Because of His sacrificial love, we have the example and encouragement to do the same:

- We rejoice for others' victories.
- We sing praises for their blessings.
- We weep for their pain and loss.

TO GO . . .

See how Psalm 103 reveals God's love and compassion. As you go, ask God to make you more compassionate and loving to your family.

As you build yourselves up in your most holy faith, praying in the Holy Spirit, keep yourselves in the love of God, waiting expectantly for the mercy of our Lord Jesus Christ for eternal life. (Jude 20–21)

"Keep an eye on my puppy so she doesn't run away."

"Keep that hammer away from small kids."

"Keep your money in a safe place."

When we *keep* something, we're guarding it or making sure it's safe. You've had to keep up with school supplies, keys, a phone, or even younger siblings.

Jude's letter uses this same concept of keeping as a way to build up our faith: "Keep yourselves in the love of God." That might seem like a strange command, knowing that God's love is strong and eternal and always with us.

But, are you . . .

- aware of His love?
- spreading His love to others?
- changed by His love?

God's love is always there, but we're likely to forget it or ignore it if we don't choose to keep it fresh in our minds and our hearts.

TO GO . . .

Read all of the book of Jude; it's only one chapter! As you go, write "God loves me" somewhere you'll see it several times.

31 FORGIVENESS

Just as the Lord has forgiven you, so you are also to forgive. (Colossians 3:13)

Jesus' followers are called to forgive. You knew that.

But we often assign standards to our forgiveness: "I'll forgive if she apologizes." "I'll forgive when I'm not angry." Or sometimes we go as far as to say, "I will never forgive that." And even if you think maybe you should forgive someone, the world likely will tell you forgiveness is optional. You'll hear people say, "If you don't stand up for yourself, they'll just do it again," or "Some people just don't deserve forgiveness."

That's not what the Bible says, though. We are instructed to forgive as Jesus forgave us. And how was that? He forgave us . . .

- while we were still sinners.
- when we didn't deserve it.
- completely.
- honestly.
- without any standards.

When you first came to Jesus and confessed your sins, He was, in essence, saying to you, "You were already forgiven." He forgave you when He died on the cross. Can you forgive like that?

TO GO . . .

Read this entire passage in Colossians 3:12–17. As you go, ask God to help you understand the depth and fullness of His forgiveness for you.

And be kind and compassionate to one another, forgiving one another, just as God also forgave you in Christ. (Ephesians 4:32)

You've seen it before: some little kids are playing and one kid hurts the other. The hurt kid goes crying off to his mother to tattle and the offender to his mother to defend himself.

The mothers try to end the conflict. So, the mother of the instigator instructs him, "Go apologize." And the mother of the hurt one says, "Tell him you forgive him." Both boys comply with scowled faces and crossed arms. They may have said the words, but their hearts just aren't there.

That's not what forgiveness should look like. Paul even went so far as to explain that our forgiveness should also include kindness and compassion.

How should that look?

- The offender is humbled and genuinely repentant.
- The offended is honest and gracious.
- Both parties yield the situation to God, believing He forgave us in this manner.

Spiritual maturity includes merciful forgiveness.

TO GO . . .

The featured verse starts with "And." Look at Ephesians 4:31 to see what came before it. As you go, check your attitude. Does your forgiveness include kindness?

33 FORGIVENESS

> *Let the wicked one abandon his way and the sinful one his thoughts; let him return to the LORD, so he may have compassion on him, and to our God, for he will freely forgive. (Isaiah 55:7)*

If you are old enough to read these words, you are old enough to remember a time when you were wicked. That may sound harsh, but consider the qualities of a wicked person: Guilty of a crime and hostile to God. That describes every single person who has ever walked the earth.

We have all been wicked because we have all been guilty of sin and consciously, intentionally chosen against God's law, but that's not the end of the story. When we agree with God that we are wicked, He has compassion on us and freely forgives us as many times as we need.

Returning to God is more than saying I'm sorry; it includes . . .

- agreeing with God that we sinned.
- believing our sin was against God and ultimately against ourselves.
- choosing not to sin again.

TO GO . . .

The same Hebrew word for *wicked* is in Psalm 1:1. See if you can find it. As you go, ask God to give you the faith to believe He has forgiven you.

*Then I acknowledged my sin to you and did not concealed my iniquity. I said, "I will confess my transgressions to the L*ORD*," and you forgave the guilt of my sin. (Psalm 32:5)*

Few things make us feel worse than trying to hide our sin. It makes us anxious, tired, and guilty.

- We hide it from others, pretending we aren't guilty.
- We hide it from ourselves, pretending it wasn't sinful or that it's not a big deal.
- We hide it from God, pretending He doesn't know or doesn't care.

Hiding our sin will never lead to peace or forgiveness; we will never cover our sin to the point that it is gone. In fact, pretending our sin doesn't exist only makes matters worse.

But confession removes the power of sin! How? Through confession, we are open with ourselves and with God. We accept that He is God, we are not, and we disobeyed.

Confession opens the pathway between us and God, clearing out the clutter of sin.

TO GO . . .

Read the other benefits of confessing in the rest of Psalm 32. As you go, confess to God one sin you've already committed today. How does it feel, knowing you're forgiven?

"And whenever you stand praying, if you have anything against anyone, forgive him, so that your Father in heaven will also forgive you your wrongdoing." (Mark 11:25)

Quick review: God is all-powerful, all-knowing, and all-loving. He has complete authority over everything. Therefore, He gets to make the rules.

One of God's rules is this: forgive. Why? Because when we choose to NOT forgive someone, we're playing God, pretending we have the authority to declare a person guilty. That's not our call; it's God's.

God doesn't mess around with unforgiveness. In Mark 11:25, Jesus taught that we can become aware of our own unforgiveness even in the middle of our prayers. Why is that? Because when we're close to God, seeking Him, He will bring to mind the things that keep us from Him. That includes unforgiveness.

So pray:

- *God, who has wronged me?*
- *Who am I jealous of?*
- *Who rubs me the wrong way?*

You can do it! Wherever you are right now, forgive.

TO GO . . .

Look at Hebrews 8:12, and see how it relates to the above verse. As you go, don't just settle for half-hearted forgiveness; ask God to help you forgive fully!

Though your sins are scarlet, they will be as white as snow; though they are crimson red, they will be like wool. (Isaiah 1:18)

What's your favorite color? Not just "red" or "green" or "blue." Is it turquoise? Burnt orange? Pomegranate red? Dark chocolate brown?

People can be passionate about colors they love (or detest). And if you read the Bible carefully, you'll notice several specific colors mentioned by God Himself.

The color red holds special significance in God's Word. Symbolizing blood, it points to . . .

- the ongoing sacrifices made to cover sin.
- the lasting sacrifice of Jesus, which eternally redeems us from our sin.

Each sin you commit is visible to God. Sin is like the dark, rich color of blood. Each person who ever lived has sinned, and the red of those sins leaves a stain *unless* it's been forgiven. When the blood of Jesus comes in contact with our sin-stained lives, we are made perfectly, beautifully white.

TO GO . . .

Read more about the power in Jesus' blood in Ephesians 1:3–10. As you go, ask God to help you see that sin has stained you. Praise Him for His forgiveness!

"And forgive us our debts, as we also have forgiven our debtors." (Matthew 6:12)

Many people read Matthew 6:12 and think it's talking about money. Technically, it can mean money, but that's not all. It's actually talking about some sort of gratitude or obligation owed to someone.

Consider a few examples:

- You loaned a shirt to a friend and he stained it. You expect him to replace it.
- Your little sister used your bed for a nap and left it a wreck. You want the bed made.
- A kid you barely know said something crude about you; you expect an apology.

In each of these cases, you are owed a debt. At the same time, you owe a debt to God: the debt of disobedience, the debt of unbelief . . . simply put, the debt of sin.

Jesus explains very clearly how the two are related: we forgive others what they owe us, and God forgives us what we owe Him. God forgives freely; we can (and should) do the same.

TO GO . . .

You'll probably recognize this verse in a famous prayer in Matthew 6:9–13. As you go, think of a person in your life that owes you. Choose to forgive that person, no strings attached.

Peter . . . asked, "Lord, how many times shall I forgive my brother or sister . . . ? As many as seven times?" "I tell you, not as many as seven," Jesus replied, "but seventy times seven." (Matthew 18:21–22)

Most people will forgive someone at least once. Maybe even twice. But after we've been wronged more than three times, we're probably not going to trust that person anymore.

It seems that Peter wanted permission to stop forgiving someone; he asked if seven times would be okay. That seems more than reasonable to us, right? We are rarely *that* generous.

But Jesus wasn't going to let Peter—or us—off the hook that easily. It's as though He said, "Keep counting until you get to seventy . . . times seven."

Why that number?

- It's so much more than society expects.
- It's more than you'll probably ever count.
- It's more than you've ever forgiven.

Keep forgiving until you lose count. That's when our forgiveness looks like God's forgiveness.

TO GO . . .

Jesus tells a parable that goes along with this teaching. Read it in Matthew 18:23–35. As you go, start counting the sins you've committed against God. Thank Him for His unending forgiveness.

The one who conceals his sins will not prosper,
but whoever confesses and renounces them will
find mercy. (Proverbs 28:13)

You've concealed that hole in your shirt; no big deal. You've tried to conceal that pimple on your nose; that's okay.

Concealing your sins? That's a bad plan. Why?

- Your family, friends, mentors, and leaders aren't fooled; they see you.
- God isn't fooled either; He is all-knowing and always full of love, even when we sin.
- You're the only one fooled, tricking yourself into thinking it's not a big deal or that it can stay hidden.

As followers of Jesus, the Holy Spirit nudges us when we sin; it's His job. The intent is to prompt us to confess and ask forgiveness. Many times, though, we choose to try to bury that sin, instead.

God wants us to live in honesty: with others, with ourselves, and most of all with Him. So, in order to walk honestly, we confess our sins to ourselves and to God and, when needed, to others.

Don't hide that sin; carry it straight to Him in prayer, confident in His promised mercy.

TO GO . . .

Psalm 32:5 also talks about the nasty effects of concealing sin. As you go, consider journaling your confessions to God. Beside them, ask for forgiveness.

"For this is my blood of the covenant, which is poured out for many for the forgiveness of sins." (Matthew 26:28)

From the very first sin, God made it clear that obedience was a big deal. Adam and Eve broke the only rule God had given them, and because of that, their relationship with Him and with each other was broken. God covered their bodies and their sin by the blood of a slain animal.

Throughout the next several thousand years, the blood of animals was used to cover sins—temporarily. Family heads and priests offered these blood sacrifices so that people would be forgiven for their sins, but those sacrifices lasted only until the next sin.

God had a plan, though: one that would not require ongoing sacrifices.

- Jesus would be the perfect sacrifice.
- His blood would cover all sin forever.
- He gave it freely.

Jesus spoke the words of Matthew 26:28 the night He was betrayed. In less than a day, He would be crucified. He knew His purpose and understood His role in ending the power of sin forever.

TO GO . . .

Look at Genesis 3 and find the first sacrifice offered for sin. As you go, thank Jesus for His eternal forgiveness.

Now without faith it is impossible to please God, since the one who draws near to him must believe that he exists and that he rewards those who seek him. (Hebrews 11:6)

If you've been to church, you've heard the word *faith*. There's a good chance you know what it means, but let's observe what we can just from this one verse:

- It takes faith to please God.
- It takes faith to believe God exists.
- It takes faith to seek God.
- It takes faith to believe God rewards us.

This is not the complete definition of faith, but it contains a truth that even many mature Christians don't understand: you can't please God without believing that He is who He says He is. No matter how many commandments you obey, how many good things you do, or how many bad things you don't do, it is our active faith that pleases God.

Believing God is where faith begins, and faith pleases Him. Seek Him and find Him by faith!

TO GO . . .

Read about other people whose faith made them famous in Hebrews 11:5–40. As you go, make a list of who God is. Ask yourself, *Do I believe this about God?*

So faith comes from what is heard, and what is heard comes through the message about Christ. (Romans 10:17)

What have you heard today? There has been a lot of noise in your life: voices, music, advertisements, people online, even the beeps from your phone.

Have you heard from God, though?

If you have chosen to believe that Jesus is your Savior and your Lord, you have faith. It took faith to believe in Him and to choose to follow Him. In the same manner, our faith is strengthened when we hear truth *about* Jesus. The more we hear about Jesus, the more we can hear *from* Jesus.

So here's the question again: Have you heard from God today? *No,* you might be thinking. *He hasn't spoken.*

But He has. For thousands of years, God spoke words to His people; those words are now for us. Faithful men wrote them down and collected them together through the years. Every word points to the truth about Jesus, and every time we hear those words, our faith grows stronger.

TO GO . . .

Choose one paragraph in Romans to believe today. As you go, find a song to listen to that speaks truth about God and Jesus.

Now faith is the reality of what is hoped for, the proof of what is not seen. (Hebrews 11:1)

Do you see the word *reality* in Hebrews 11:1? Some other Bibles may use the words *assurance*, *substance*, *being sure*, *fundamental fact*, or *confidence* to translate the depth of this Greek word.

But this noun has its root meaning in a real-life application: it means "foundation." It's the primary thing that makes for a firm, level place for the building above it. It's like the chassis of your car or the concrete and steel under your house: everything rests on that foundation, and it gives everything its stability.

A foundation . . .

- gives firmness, courage, and steadiness.
- supports everything on top of it.
- is the strongest part of a structure.

So, according to Hebrews 11:1, your faith is the foundation of your hope—meaning that your faith in Jesus is what gives you confidence in His promises. We lay a strong foundation only when we know what the Bible says and choose to believe it.

TO GO . . .

Find out how ancient this concept is by reading Hebrews 11:2. As you go, look at the foundation of each building you enter today. Let it challenge you to consider your foundation of faith.

For you are saved by grace through faith, and this is not from yourselves; it is God's gift—not from works, so that no one can boast. (Ephesians 2:8–9)

For some Christians, faith gives them anxiety. They think:

- *I just don't have enough faith.*
- *I don't know what to believe.*
- *What if I don't pray or believe in the right way?*

What if the truth is that none of these questions will ever strengthen your faith?

It's true: you have faith, but that faith is not dependent upon you; it's all on God.

Paul told the church in Ephesus, "You are saved by grace through faith, and . . . it is God's gift." God, because He loves you so much and delights in giving gifts to His children, gave you the gift of faith. It wasn't your strength, your power, or your brain that believed; it was all God.

He will hold you up when your faith wavers. It's not on you; it's on God alone. Believe His gift is perfect for you.

TO GO . . .

Read the entire paragraph in Ephesians 2:1–10. As you go, see if you can create an image that reflects the truth of today's verses.

For we walk by faith, not by sight.
(2 Corinthians 5:7)

Throughout the Bible, you'll find some examples of what it means to walk with God:

- "Enoch walked with God 300 years. . . ." (Genesis 5:22)
- "Noah was a righteous man. . . . Noah walked with God." (Genesis 6:9)
- "Love the LORD your God, walk in all his ways, keep his commands." (Joshua 22:5)

As you guessed, the idea of walking does not mean the literal picking up and putting down of your feet, but instead refers to the fullness of *how* you live. If you look like a great Christian at church but nothing like it at school, you're walking in dishonesty. If you walk like a loving kid at home but are unkind to your friends, your walk isn't genuine.

It's a little frightening to walk by faith; how can we be sure of who God is? What do we do when we're confused? Which way do we turn?

When you start asking God these questions, you're walking by faith. Follow the God who will walk with you.

TO GO . . .

Look up the examples above and learn what it means to walk with God. As you go, ponder the above verse each time you walk today.

My speech and my preaching were not
with persuasive words of wisdom but with
a demonstration of the Spirit's power.
(1 Corinthians 2:4)

Being sick isn't fun; not only do you feel bad, but sometimes, because you're contagious, you also can't even be around your friends and family.

Germs aren't the only things that are contagious; so is faith. Maybe not in the medical sense, but the more faith you see the more faith you desire for yourself. You know that's true: when you're at church camp or around other believers for a while, you tend to have a stronger faith than when you're all alone.

Paul's speech and preaching spread contagiously to the believers in Corinth. Likewise, you should surround yourself with people who truly know and believe Jesus; let their faith rub off on you. But be sure to let your faith spread to the people around you:

- friends and family
- believers and unbelievers
- younger and older

TO GO . . .

Look at what prompted Paul to say this in 1 Corinthians 2:1–5. As you go, thank God for the people whose faith has strengthened your own.

But someone will say, "You have faith, and I have works." Show me your faith without works, and I will show you faith by my works. (James 2:18)

Beware: this verse has led to many arguments between Christians. Today's verse actually sounds like James is in an argument already.

But let's look at it as friends, okay?

We have two aspects here: faith and works.

- Faith is believing who God says He is, in the form of the Father, the Son, and the Spirit.
- Works are obedience to God's instructions.

Some people believed that faith was the key to salvation; others believed it was works. Which is the answer?

Both! We start our journey with God (through Jesus) by faith: believing in His truth. But if our faith stops in our mind, it hasn't really changed us. If it doesn't change us, do we really believe it?

If your mom tells you the soup is scalding hot but you take a big bite anyway, did you really believe her?

TO GO . . .

Read all of James 2. (It's only twenty-six verses.) As you go, ask God to help you believe and to give you the faith to live in obedience.

The apostles said to the Lord, "Increase our faith."
(Luke 17:5)

It's a glorious day when you realize you can ask for more of something and get it. Whether it's a refill of your favorite drink, extra pickles on your burger, or bacon cooked extra crispy, we feel special and privileged when we get the extras for free.

Did you know that Jesus loves to give us more?

Jesus had been teaching His disciples about forgiveness and their response was, "Increase our faith." We can take a lesson from them and do the same.

Need help in any of these areas?

- "I struggle to love this difficult person."
- "I struggle to share my faith in Jesus."
- "I struggle to read my Bible and pray."
- "I struggle with believing I am who God says I am."

Take your struggle to Jesus and ask Him to increase your faith! Granted, more faith isn't going to just fall on your head, but He will give you the opportunity to know Him better and believe Him more deeply.

TO GO . . .

Jesus said more about faith in Luke 17:6–10. As you go, ask Jesus to show you the areas where you need more faith.

> *Jesus said to him, "If you can? Everything is possible for the one who believes." Immediately the father of the boy cried out, "I do believe; help my unbelief!" (Mark 9:23–24)*

Do you get tired of perfect images, perfect social media accounts, and perfect lives?

We crave honest, real relationships. So does Jesus. He loves it when His children are honest with themselves and honest with Him. We can only imagine his joy when a man, struggling to believe Jesus, said the words: "I do believe; help my unbelief!"

You've been there!

- You know Jesus says you are loved, forgiven, and a new creation, but you don't live like it.
- You've heard Jesus died for your sins, and yet, you still sin. Where is the power over sin?
- You've been told Jesus is with you always. What about when you feel alone or afraid?

Don't pretend your faith is perfect; no one has that. Instead, make an honest statement about what you believe and back it up with an honest confession that you could really use more faith.

TO GO . . .

Read the whole story in Mark 9:14–29. As you go, have a conversation with yourself: where do you pretend to have faith?

This is the victory that has conquered the world: our faith. Who is the one who conquers the world but the one who believes that Jesus is the Son of God? (1 John 5:4–5)

If there was ever a verse to memorize deep in your heart, this is the one: it gives the secret for conquering the world.

A long time ago, there was a television cartoon called *Pinky and the Brain*, where two research mice would sneak out of their cages each night in an attempt to "take over the world." This isn't what the Bible is talking about, of course. Instead, it's talking about the ability not to let the world's sins, idols, and temptations triumph over your heart.

Our faith conquers the world, and here's the primary statement of our faith: "Jesus is the Son of God."

Consider the impact of that statement:

- Jesus has the authority of God.
- Jesus holds the power of God.
- Jesus has ultimate access to God.
- Jesus is sent by God and glorifies God.

TO GO . . .

Read more about the victory of Jesus in 1 Corinthians 15:54–57. As you go, memorize 1 John 5:5. Repeat it every day this week as you etch it on your heart.

Rejoice in hope; be patient in affliction; be persistent in prayer. (Romans 12:12)

Sometimes, the Christian life might seem like just a list of things to do and not do. God loves us and knows what is best for us. Obeying Him is critical. But we're also supposed to thrive, living with abundant joy, patience, and hope.

In today's passage, Paul listed three things that Jesus' followers can do to glorify God. More than just a list of things to do, these instructions point to the depths of our hearts and minds. When we consider these three commands, we are reminded of . . .

- who God is.
- the unlimited nature of His power.
- the need to trust in His plan.

The word used for *rejoice* in Romans 12:12 is the same used in Matthew 2:10, where the wise men "saw the star . . . [and] they were overwhelmed with joy." They were thrilled because they found what they had been searching for.

We can rejoice too! We found Jesus: our Savior, Lord, and King.

TO GO . . .

Look at what else the wise men did in Matthew 2:9–12. As you go, consider three things that God gives that brings you hope for today, the future, and eternity.

When I am filled with cares, your comfort brings me joy. (Psalm 94:19)

Are you filled with cares? Most people care, or worry, about something. They worry about:

- safety
- money
- the future
- health

Sometimes people might say, "I don't have a care in the world." Sounds great, right? But it's a little unrealistic. Our world is sin-filled; the future is uncertain; and we rarely have the knowledge we need to make the best decisions. We are concerned for our own lives, the people we love, and even people we may not know but whose lives are filled with very real needs.

We would actually be unaware or love less if we didn't have concern for them. So how do we offset legitimate cares?

The answer is God. He is the only source of true comfort and lasting peace in a challenging world. When life is overwhelming and our plans, struggles, and lists are more than we can handle, God offers peace and joy. We receive it when we turn over our list of cares to Him.

TO GO . . .

Read all of Psalm 94. If the psalmist can find joy in God's comfort, you can too! As you go, make a list of cares you have. Use that list as your prayer list tonight.

You reveal the path of life to me; in your presence is abundant joy; at your right hand are eternal pleasures. (Psalm 16:11)

When you have an abundance of something, you have:

- fullness
- satisfaction
- all you need

Like sitting down to your favorite meal and eating until you've had your fill, you can find joy that fills us up and satisfies. That joy is found in the presence of God.

"But I can't be at church or studying my Bible all the time," you might think. This is true, but God's presence is not only limited to times of worship or Bible study.

You can walk in His presence by keeping your mind aware of His will for you and opportunities to love others. You can stay in His presence by turning your heart towards the needs of others and how you can make Him known.

Whether you're at home, school, work, or other activities, your heart and mind can be made aware of God, which will help you to truly know abundant joy.

TO GO . . .

Learn more about abundant joy in Deuteronomy 16:15 and 2 Corinthians 8:2. As you go, write "joy" on the back of your hand as a reminder to remain in God's presence.

Rejoice always, pray constantly, give thanks in everything; for this is God's will for you in Christ Jesus. (1 Thessalonians 5:16–18)

In today's passage, we see three commands: rejoice, pray, and give thanks. These sound like good things for believers to do, right? But did you notice what Paul put next to them? They almost make the commands impossible to follow: always, constantly, in everything.

Was Paul serious? Are we really supposed to rejoice, pray, and give thanks in the ugly, the sad, the horrible, and the tragic? Should we give thanks for death and disease? Should we rejoice when people suffer? Should we pray when everything seems out of control?

Yes. And even though it seems crazy to rejoice, pray, and give thanks when you're stressed, sad, or overwhelmed, it is possible. Pause and consider Jesus:

- He loves you.
- He knows what is going on.
- He is in control.

Only Jesus can empower you to find joy, prayer, and thankfulness in every situation.

TO GO . . .

Read this verse in context by looking at 1 Thessalonians 5:12–22. As you go, choose to rejoice, pray, and give thanks in the good as well as the stressful situations.

> *"Until now you have asked for nothing in my name. Ask and you will receive, so that your joy may be complete." (John 16:24)*

What does "in my name" mean in John 16:24? Here's an illustration: If your mom sent you to the store to get a loaf of bread, she's expecting you to represent her while carrying out her wishes. You get the bread on your mom's behalf, or "in her name."

When we ask something in Jesus' name, we ask for something that reflects His character and is in His will. Now, that's tricky: it's hard to know what the will of Jesus is. Or is it?

We can be sure He always wants us to . . .

- love.
- forgive.
- be gracious.
- show mercy.

When was the last time you asked for one of these things? Instead of praying, "Lord, please let _____ happen," try, "Lord, please help me show love and grace, no matter what."

Try it! Our joy is complete when we pray in Jesus' name.

TO GO . . .

Bible verses are best read in context, so read John 16:16–24. As you go, choose one thing you know is Jesus' will for you. Pray for that each time you pray today.

A person takes joy in giving an answer; and a timely word—how good that is! (Proverbs 15:23)

If you made a list of things that bring you joy, you might say:

- friends
- great weather for the game
- canceled tests
- sleeping in
- finding $5 you forgot about in your jacket.

But Proverbs 15:23 gives something else to bring you joy: giving an answer. Words are powerful; not only can they harm, but they can also bring great joy to both the speaker and the hearer.

When was the last time you said something to someone and it made you truly joyous? Words that bring joy are wise, God-glorifying, full of love, and honest. Whether it's someone asking for advice, looking for ideas, or even needing help, your answer can bring joy!

Don't think so? Try it. Check your sarcasm, grumpiness, or whatever attitude keeps you from giving an answer that points to God's love. Choose to speak words that give joy to yourself and others.

TO GO . . .

Look at 1 Peter 3:15 to find out what else you can share with others through your words. As you go, ask God to give you joy as you speak words that point others to Him.

Rejoice with those who rejoice; weep with those who weep. (Romans 12:15)

You've probably experienced it: you have great news and you share it with a friend or family member with tons of excitement. They, however, only respond with negativity, focusing on their own issues. Or worse, maybe it was you who ruined the excitement of someone else's good news.

Sometimes we struggle to be happy for people whose lives are going well. Why? Well, maybe:

- We're jealous.
- We're resentful of their good fortune.
- We've fixed our eyes on our own struggles.

When we miss the opportunity to rejoice with others, we miss out on one of the greatest blessings of friends and families. Rejoicing comes when we trust God to meet our needs and bless us, even when it pales in comparison to someone else's life.

Jealousy chokes out joy because our comparison to others makes everything a competition. We are each blessed in dozens of ways every day; the more aware we are of our own blessings, the more we can rejoice with those who are also rejoicing.

TO GO . . .

Find other reasons to rejoice with others in Psalm 122:1 and Philippians 2:17–18. As you go, make a mental (or written) list of ten blessings in your own life.

I have no greater joy than this: to hear that my children are walking in truth. (3 John 4)

These words were written by the apostle John. By the time he wrote them, he was a very old man. According to tradition, he was the last of the twelve disciples who lived with Jesus during His earthly ministry. Because of his faith, he was exiled to an island, likely near death.

And yet in his letter he wrote the words you see above. He found joy in hearing that his children were walking in the truth. Now as far as we know, John didn't have any literal children; however, he had many spiritual children: men and women he had led to faith and discipleship.

Who are your spiritual mothers and fathers? It may be your mother or father, but perhaps it's a:

- youth pastor
- godly teacher
- mentor
- extended family member
- older friend

Whoever it is, you bring them joy when they hear that you know and walk in the truth of God.

TO GO . . .

Read all of 3 John. (It's only one chapter!) As you go, call or send a text to a spiritual mother or father, telling them how God's Word is changing you.

> *"I have told you these things so that my joy may be in you and your joy may be complete."* (John 15:11)

Jesus spoke these words to His disciples. Can you picture Him in your head? Often the image we get of Jesus is a bearded man who is serious, solemn, and maybe even sour. But here, Jesus speaks of His joy!

Jesus had the joy of . . .

- being fully known by God.
- identifying as God's child.
- knowing heaven is real and wonderful.
- trusting God's call on His life.

Those were reasons for real, pure joy. His joy was to be in us, and our joy would be made "complete." That Greek word gives us the image of cramming something into a small space and filling it completely. It can also mean full, abounding, or finished. And when Jesus' joy becomes our joy, it fills us completely.

Like Jesus, we can know all these things and receive the joy that comes from the truth of God's Word.

TO GO . . .

See if you can determine how Psalm 16:11 ties into John 15:11. As you go, re-read the bulleted list above. Try to memorize it.

"I tell you, in the same way, there is joy in the presence of God's angels over one sinner who repents." (Luke 15:10)

When was the last time you were in the middle of a celebrating crowd? Maybe it was at a ballgame, concert, or parade? If you've been in one of these excited gatherings, you've experienced the contagious joy that is in a group of enthusiastic people.

Today's verse points to a party more intense than anything you've experienced: the celebration of angels. Just imagine these powerful, majestic beings—singing, shouting, praising.

It's surely a glorious sight.

And, according to Luke 15:10, there is a specific reason for their celebration: one repenting sinner. One person saying, "God is right and I'm going to believe Him." When you repent, you change your mind and agree with God about sin. It's more than just being sorry; it's vowing to change.

Choosing to follow Jesus as Savior demands repentance and leads to angelic celebration!

TO GO . . .

Read other instances of angels celebrating in Luke 2:13 and Job 38:7. As you go, ask God if you need to repent of something in your heart or mind.

Our Lord and God, you are worthy to receive glory and honor and power, because you have created all things, and by your will they exist and were created. (Revelation 4:11)

If you look at the words *worthy* and *worship* side by side, you'll see they both start with the same three letters. It only makes sense to note that *worship* is acknowledging that God is *worthy*.

In Revelation 4:11, John is viewing a scene in heaven. He sees:

- a throne
- God
- many colors
- all kinds of creatures
- thunder and lightning

Every attention is pointed to God. And in the midst of it, you read the words of the song they sing: God is worthy to receive glory and honor and power because He created all things and makes all things exist.

Even if He'd done nothing else, God deserves our worship for that. (Of course, He has done so, so much more!) His creation of the earth and the heavens and everything in them make Him worthy of any credit or acknowledgment.

TO GO . . .

Read about the entire scene in Revelation 4:1–11. As you go, think about the words to your favorite worship song. Dare to sing them aloud.

"God is spirit, and those who worship him must worship in Spirit and in truth." (John 4:24)

Jesus spoke the words in today's passage to a woman who lived near the Jews but didn't really understand or agree with everything the Jews believed. She had actually begun a discussion with Jesus about where the "right" place to worship God could be found.

Jesus wouldn't even entertain the thought of having only one place to worship; instead, He pointed her to the right *way* to worship God: in Spirit and in truth.

No one could (and no one will) put God into a box or assign Him a place; He is spirit, meaning He can be anywhere and can be worshiped anywhere.

What is required, though, is truth, meaning we know God through His Word, we believe what He says about Himself, and we live according to who He is.

Where you worship isn't the focus; who you worship—and what you worship about Him—is what matters.

TO GO . . .

Read the entire conversation in John 4:1–26. As you go, take time today to worship God in your car, in a class, or even in your room.

Then Abraham said to his young men, "Stay here with the donkey. The boy and I will go over there to worship; then we'll come back to you." (Genesis 22:5)

Today's passage is found in the midst of one of the most amazing stories in the Old Testament: God calling Abraham to sacrifice his son. (Spoiler alert: God was testing Abraham and didn't make him go through with it.)

Abraham had a three-day journey with some servants and all the materials they would need for the sacrifice loaded onto his donkey. But when the final climb came, Abraham told the servants to stay with the donkey so he and Isaac could "go over there to worship." You might think Abraham was lying so they wouldn't realize he was sacrificing his son.

But worship is acknowledging who God is and offering Him our best. Abraham's best and most precious thing he could offer was his son, and he was willing to lose it in order to honor God. In the same sense, we honor God by giving Him our attention, honor, and trust.

TO GO . . .

Read the whole story in Genesis 22. As you go, consider what Abraham believed about God in order to be willing to sacrifice his greatest blessing.

The people believed, and when they heard that the LORD had paid attention to them and that he had seen their misery, they knelt low and worshiped. (Exodus 4:31)

The book of Exodus tells the story of Moses and the Israelites escaping slavery in Egypt by the mighty hand of God. In today's passage, Moses and his brother, Aaron, have just met with the Israelite leaders and shown them God's plan.

We are wise to take note of the verbs in today's passage. They . . .

- believed.
- heard.
- worshiped.

For centuries, God's people—the descendants of Abraham—had suffered under the harsh rule of the Egyptians. Their hopelessness turned to worship, though, when they realized God had seen their situation and paid attention to them. Seeing Moses and Aaron come with power, authority, and a plan to free them changed everything about their situation.

What about you? Do you cry out to God with your struggles? How has God given you comfort, peace, or help lately? Have you responded with worship?

TO GO . . .

See if you can find a parallel between today's verse and Revelation 22:8. As you go, find time today to really cry out to God, admitting to Him where you're struggling.

You, Lord, are the only God. You created the
heavens, the highest heavens with all their stars
. . . You give life to all of them, and all the stars of
heaven worship you. (Nehemiah 9:6)

We can't help but worship when we truly focus on God.

At the beginning of Nehemiah 9, the Israelites have gathered and already spent many hours confessing sins, reading from the book of the law, crying out and worshiping. God had their total focus.

This is a picture of what real worship looks like:

- acknowledging who God is and who we are
- giving Him glory for what He has done
- realizing that all of creation points to Him

When we turn our minds and hearts to know God in truth, we see Him everywhere: in the stars, the land, the sea, and in every single living creature. When we look for His fingerprint, we can't help but praise Him.

TO GO . . .

Read the entire prayer in Nehemiah 9:5–37. As you go, choose a night this week to go out and look at the stars. Speak this verse aloud.

Then Job stood up, tore his robe, and shaved his head. He fell to the ground and worshiped, saying: Naked I came from my mother's womb, and naked I will leave this life. (Job 1:20–21)

You know about Job: he was a righteous man, followed God, was kind to others, had a great family and a great life. Then, God allowed Satan to take almost everything away: his flocks were stolen and his children were killed . . . total devastation.

In today's passage, Job has just heard the bad news all at once. Beginning to mourn all he had lost (by tearing his robe and shaving his head), notice what he did:

- He fell to the ground.
- He worshiped.

Loss of loved ones and wealth are not normally what would lead us to worship. Still, it's the best first step in any situation. Worship is looking at God and saying: "I know who You are and I know You are in control."

Worship is not just for the great times; it can also be for the worst.

TO GO . . .

Read the whole first chapter of Job. As you go, ask yourself, "When does worship come naturally to me? When should I worship intentionally?"

67 WORSHIP

Ascribe to the LORD the glory due his name;
worship the LORD in the splendor of his holiness.
(Psalm 29:2)

Worship has many different aspects. More than just a part of Sunday morning gatherings, worship is music, lifestyle, mind-set, or belief.

Worship can have even more aspects than just those. Today's verse gives two more aspects of worship.

Ascribing glory to His name. The Hebrew word for ascribe can mean to give, provide, set, put, or come. Our worship involves coming to him and giving attention to who He is: all-powerful, all-knowing, loving, judge, and creator.

Worshiping in the splendor of His holiness involves those things that embellish the things that set God apart. His wisdom, strength, understanding, and compassion are nothing like ours; they are higher and more intense than we could even fathom.

More than singing or quoting Scripture, worship involves knowing who God is and making Him known. That can happen through songs but also through acts of compassion, forgiveness, and kindness.

Want to get into the right mind-set and heart position for worship? Start with the two things in Psalm 29:2.

TO GO . . .

Look for the similarities to this verse in 1 Chronicles 16:29. As you go, make a mental list of the characteristics of God. Show off who He is today.

Come, let us shout joyfully to the LORD, shout triumphantly to the rock of our salvation! (Psalm 95:1)

Public worship looks different depending on the nature of the congregation. Some churches have loud volumes and big expressions; others are more reserved.

How your church praises God is not the only worship in your life; you should also have times of personal worship, as well. And it should, every now and then, be loud!

In Psalm 95:1, the psalmist is inviting people to shout joyfully. The Hebrew word he uses actually refers to a shrill, creaking, or ringing shout. You've probably done this before: when you're simply overcome with excitement, and you can't help but shout at the top of your lungs.

There's a place for this kind of worship. Maybe it's at your church. Maybe it's not. Perhaps you need to get alone or with your youth group, wherever you're more comfortable shouting to God. Wherever it is, take time—regularly—to shout your praise.

TO GO . . .

Read Psalm 95:3–5 and find reasons why you should worship joyfully. As you go, consider others who would love to worship loudly with you. Plan a worship night with them.

> *Therefore, brothers and sisters, in view of the mercies of God, I urge you to present your bodies as a living sacrifice, holy and pleasing to God; this is your true worship. (Romans 12:1)*

Worship can have many meanings:

- singing about God
- praising God
- thinking about God and who He is
- living in a way that glorifies God

The first two describe outward worship; the last two point to inward worship.

Paul was referring to both inward and outward worship in Romans 12:1: True worship is presenting our bodies as a living, holy, pleasing sacrifice to God. Unlike animal sacrifices of the Old Testament, which were killed and burned, we are living, meaning we choose to sacrifice as we go about our lives.

We *choose* to be holy in our thoughts, our words, and our actions. We *choose* to please God with our relationships, our love, and our attitudes. You are making a sacrifice when you choose to lay down your life in order to live it for God, inwardly and outwardly.

TO GO . . .

Read Romans 12:2 to see how Paul completed this thought. As you go, invite God to show you how to worship like a living sacrifice today.

He answered them, "I'm a Hebrew. I worship the
Lord, the God of the heavens, who made the sea
and the dry land." (Jonah 1:9)

Jonah is one of the most famous prophets of the Old Testament, not because of his faithfulness to God but, instead, because of what happened when he didn't obey.

We still have to give Jonah credit: he found his identity in God. Even when he was caught in a storm because he was trying to run away—literally—from God's plan for his life, he still knew, deep down, that he belonged to the Lord.

Jonah defined himself as a Hebrew, or a descendant of Abraham, who worshiped the Lord, the God of the heavens who made the sea and the dry land.

Don't miss the significance of Jonah's situation when he spoke these words: he was on the Mediterranean Sea, in a storm so great that the ship was about to break apart. In essence, Jonah was giving God credit for the storm, acknowledging His power.

Worship, at its core, is acknowledging God in every circumstance.

TO GO . . .

Read Jonah 1:1–8 to see the details of the story. As you go, acknowledge that God is in total control of your circumstances.

Guard your heart above all else, for it is the source of life. (Proverbs 4:23)

Guarding something involves protection from harm. We guard the things that are valuable, important, or powerful to us. Figuratively or literally, you probably guard your close relationships, memories, skills and talents, and cherished belongings.

How well do you guard your heart? It is the source of your emotions, beliefs, and attitudes. When your heart is in line with God's truth and compassion, you live genuinely for Him and keep your heart protected.

Do you protect your heart from sins and temptations that would corrupt or mislead it?

Do you fill your heart with the joy, peace, and love of God by knowing His Word? Do you use your heart as a reservoir of God's love and peace for others?

Do you realize that what you see, read, hear, and watch makes its way to your heart?

Like a sentry guarding a door, we guard our hearts by paying special attention to everything that enters it, knowing that what comes into our heart changes our thoughts and our lives.

TO GO . . .

Dig deeper into this topic in Philippians 4:7. As you go, choose to take one action that will guard your heart today.

"For where your treasure is, there your heart will be also." (Matthew 6:21)

What did you treasure when you were younger? Did you treasure erasers or trading cards or stickers or action figures? Maybe you treasured games or a special toy. When you treasure something, you make it a priority to keep it in your possession, keep it free from harm, and keep it in good condition.

What do you treasure now that you're older? Perhaps a few different questions will lead to that answer:

- What do you do in your free time?
- What do you think about when you're lying in bed?
- If you had 24 hours to spend $1000, what would you do?

You've just revealed your treasure. And, according to Matthew 6:21, you just revealed where your heart is. It's a good test, because we need to regularly check to make sure our heart, mind, and strength are focused on God and His Word.

If your treasure is not in God, shift your focus to Him. Learn more about His love, and let it fill you.

TO GO . . .

This verse is in the middle of Jesus teaching a sermon in Matthew 6:19–24. As you go, consider one step you can take to daily treasure God's Word.

> *Love the Lord your God with all your heart, with all your soul, and with all your strength. These words that I am giving you today are to be in your heart. (Deuteronomy 6:5–6)*

You might think that loving God most means loving others less. That seems mathematically true, but in God's equation, it's not.

Human love is flawed; we're surrounded and influenced by sin, pride, and worldliness. But when we love God fully, He puts His love in our hearts! His love, unlike ours, is pure and best. Basically, we trade our lacking love for God's amazing love, and that's what we are able to give to others.

What does it take to give God love?

- all our heart
- all our soul
- all our strength

If that seems extreme, consider that God is offering you the most amazing trade ever: your love for His love! We love Him with our time, our influence, our focus, our attitudes, and our passions. He fills us with His love, which we share with others.

TO GO . . .

Deuteronomy 6:4–9 is one of the most repeated passages in all of the Law. Consider memorizing it. As you go, consider how you are loving God with your heart, soul, and strength today.

Now Ezra had determined in his heart to study the law of the Lord, obey it, and teach its statutes and ordinances in Israel. (Ezra 7:10)

Does your heart speak to you? It's not really loud; sometimes it's like a whisper or a sigh. But maybe you've heard it speak when you . . .

- heard a missionary speak about loving orphans.
- watched a video about helping hurting people.
- read about a need in your community or around the world.

Sometimes, though, our hearts can be grumpy, hard, or simply evil. But when we've devoted our hearts to knowing God and following Him, the Holy Spirit leads our hearts in the way we should go.

How can you know if God is leading your heart to do something? Ask, "Would this bring glory to me or to God?" "Does this help me love others?" "Am I going to know God better through this?"

Ezra, an Old Testament hero, knew his heart was telling him to study, obey, and teach God's Word.

What is your heart telling you?

TO GO . . .

Have your Bible? See what Proverbs 5:13 and Romans 6:17 say about obeying and teaching God's Word. As you go, spend five minutes in silence. Ask the Spirit to speak to your heart.

75 *HEART*

Who put wisdom in the heart or gave the mind understanding? (Job 38:36)

The last few chapters of Job are some of the most powerful words describing God. Chapter 38 begins with the words, "Then the Lᴏʀᴅ answered Job from the whirlwind . . ." and for the next three chapters, God speaks to Job—describing His power and knowledge.

Imagine yourself in Job's position. God is speaking to you from a whirlwind; everything around you is loud, swirling, and intense. God's voice is booming, and He asks, "Who put wisdom in the heart?"

It's a rhetorical question; one asked to make a point rather than one asked to get an answer. God alone puts wisdom in the heart.

The deeper question, then, is this: is your heart wise? Wisdom that comes from God . . .

- acknowledges God's sovereignty.
- forgives, hopes, and is patient and loving.
- points to God's strength and power, bringing Him glory.

Are you living according to your heart's wisdom?

TO GO . . .

Read all of Job 38. If you have time, go to the end of the book. It will be worth it! As you go, commit to digging out the wisdom that God has placed in your heart.

*You have put more joy in my heart than they have
when their grain and new wine abound. (Psalm 4:7)*

Psalm 4, written by King David, is given the title, "A Night Prayer." It contains the words, "on your bed, reflect in your heart and be still" (v. 4). It's an insightful look into what David may have pondered while trying to sleep at night.

This question is posed to him: "Who can show us anything good?" You've probably heard a similar statement from people around you:

- "The world is a mess."
- "Governments are corrupt."
- "People are evil."
- "Everything is going downhill."

But for those of us who know and love and experience God, we don't fall for those lies. Why? Because we've experienced the joy that God puts in our heart.

His joy is not dependent upon situations or circumstances. His joy comes from who He is, what He does, how He works, and the hope for today, tomorrow, and forever.

TO GO . . .

Read all of the Night Prayer in Psalm 4. Read it again just before you go to sleep tonight. As you go, find one person who sees nothing good in the world. Share God's joy today.

My heart says this about you: "Seek his face."
Lᴏʀᴅ, I will seek your face. (Psalm 27:8)

We can fill our hearts with lies or truth, pride or humility, God or self.

Our hearts contain the combinations of our thoughts, our personalities, and our emotions; therefore, our hearts are the center of who we are and what we do. When our hearts get a taste of God, we realize we are at our best when we are complete in Him.

And your heart whispers, "Seek his face." It's like you're looking for someone in a crowd; you see a person that looks like Him, but you're not sure; so you try to get a closer look.

That's what our hearts desperately desire: to know the real God.

So what does it mean to seek God's face? It means . . .

- knowing His identity according to the Bible.
- believing what He says and obeying.
- living according to the love of Jesus.
- showing others God in everything you do.

TO GO . . .

See what Psalm 24:6 and 2 Chronicles 7:14 say about seeking God's face. As you go, read over the bulleted list again. Which of these have you been neglecting?

For God is greater than our hearts, and he knows all things. (1 John 3:20)

Your heart . . .

- calls you to know God.
- contains joy from God.
- has the potential to be wise.
- controls and directs you.

So what do you do when you look down deep and realize your heart is a mess? You turn it over to the One who has power over your heart: God.

Sometimes we have so much guilt, shame, and sin in our hearts that we feel overwhelmed. Our hearts whisper, "You deserve it," "You are worthless," or some other condemnation. But those are not the words of God! God says, "You are mine." "You are loved." "I am here for you."

Don't believe a deceptive heart. God is greater! Fill your mind with His Word and let it saturate your heart. Let His love and truth bring you comfort.

TO GO . . .

Have your Bible? See what Jeremiah 17:9 teaches about the heart. As you go, whisper to God that you trust Him to take charge of your heart. Let Him have it.

You also must be patient. Strengthen your hearts, because the Lord's coming is near. (James 5:8)

Strengthening your heart sounds like a good idea to most believers.

But what does that even mean? Well, let's pretend you wanted to strengthen your legs. You could think about getting stronger. You could make plans to get stronger. You could hire a trainer or buy a book about strengthening your legs, but none of those things would actually work; only exercise would get the job done.

Sometimes people make the same mistake about their hearts: they attempt to make their hearts stronger through thinking, planning, reading, or getting a mentor. But just like strengthening those legs, nothing works aside from actually working the muscles.

So, how do you strengthen your heart?

- Love the one who needs a friend.
- Serve someone who can't repay.
- Forgive someone who never said, "I'm sorry."
- Help a person without their knowing it.
- Care for someone who is helpless.
- Smile at a person having a tough time.

TO GO . . .

See what 2 Thessalonians 2:16–17 says about strengthening your heart. As you go, choose two items from the bulleted list above to do as a heart exercise today.

For the word of God is living and effective and sharper than any doubled-edged sword. . . . It is able to judge the thoughts and intentions of the heart. (Hebrews 4:12)

When you were little, there was always an adult around to break up fights and settle arguments. You needed someone for that. But as you get older, you'll find that many of your biggest struggles are with yourself:

- What path do I take?
- Which relationships do I keep? Which do I let go?
- Where do I pour my time, energy, and money?
- What is the right thing to do?

Growing up is tricky; you don't always know exactly what to do in every situation.

But in spiritual matters, there is one authority: God's Word. According to Hebrews 4:12 it is sharp and it is able to judge our hearts. When you're uncertain, unbalanced, or unaware, God's Word is the place to turn.

TO GO . . .

See if you can find the parallel between today's verse and 1 Peter 1:23. As you go, choose one book of the Bible to start reading from daily.

Do not be conformed to this age, but be transformed by the renewing of your mind, so that you may discern what is the good, pleasing, and perfect will of God. (Romans 12:2)

Look at those two words that end similarly: *conformed* and *transformed*.

- Conformed means that you are changed by something. You become more like the things around you.
- Transformed means you actually become a new creation from the inside out.

Obviously, transforming is what we want as followers to Jesus. We don't want to be like our pre-Jesus selves; we want to be renewed by Him!

Transforming into a Jesus-follower doesn't happen automatically, though: we have to renew our minds in order to be transformed.

Picture a tree. In order for it to grow and be healthy, it needs sun, water, nutrients, and protection. Similarly, our minds need to take in things that make it healthy and strong. We get that from the Word of God. It takes ongoing, daily time in the Bible to reach a true transformation.

TO GO . . .

See what Ephesians 4:23 and Psalm 19:7 add to the concept of renewing. As you go, be on the lookout for ideas and beliefs that are not of God.

For those who live according to the flesh have their minds set on the things of the flesh, but those who live according to the Spirit have their minds set on the things of the Spirit. (Romans 8:5)

You've heard people make statements insinuating that their minds are separate from their actions:

- "That kind of violent movie doesn't affect me."
- "I know that song sounds rough, but I just like the beat."
- "My parents think I'm not mature enough for this type of book, but I'm fine."

Granted, we're not eternally corrupted by observing sinful things one time. However, we are definitely shaped by the things we repeatedly put in our minds. And when we repeatedly think about things that feed our worldly selves, we eventually start to live them out.

On the other hand, if we feed our minds with the Holy Spirit, our lives will follow. Those things include God's Word, loving others, living in truth, and being compassionate.

TO GO . . .

Read Paul's entire thought in Romans 8:1–11. As you go, write the word *mind-set* where it'll pop out at you. Let it remind you to keep your mind set on the things of the Spirit.

And the peace of God, which surpasses all
understanding, will guard your hearts and minds
in Christ Jesus. (Philippians 4:7)

Your mind is in a battle and you might not even know it.

So many things can attack your mind: worries, stress, lies, doubts, and countless other things. Sometimes people say, "My mind just gets carried away when I get scared." Yours probably does that, too.

But there is a protection offered; the peace of God is that protection. Most people hear about God's peace and shake their heads. "That's crazy," they say. "How can anybody have peace in this crazy world?"

Well, according to today's verse, it "surpasses all understanding," which means we won't ever really be able to answer *how* God's peace is there; we just know that *it is*. We can have peace because . . .

- God is near.
- God is love.
- God is almighty.
- God is aware.

When Jesus is your Lord and Savior, the peace of God is yours to protect your heart and mind.

TO GO . . .

See what else you can learn about God's peace in Romans 5:1 and Romans 15:13. As you go, choose one of the items from the bulleted list above and meditate on it.

"As for you, Solomon my son, know the God of your father, and serve him wholeheartedly and with a willing mind." (1 Chronicles 28:9)

King David had a son, Solomon, who would be king after David died. That wouldn't be his only responsibility: he was also charged with building the temple of God in Jerusalem.

Today's passage is found in the middle of David's speech to Solomon and all the leaders who would help in the multi-year building project. It would require many workers, supplies, years of planning, and knowledge.

So what were David's first and most important instructions?

- Know God.
- Serve God with your heart and mind.

David had walked with God for many years. He knew that God was not concerned with an outward display of obedience as much as He wanted a heart and mind that knew Him and wanted to bring Him glory. Every job requires knowledge of God and complete surrender to Him.

Your first goal should be to know and serve God.

TO GO . . .

Read more of King David's speech in 1 Chronicles 28. As you go, commit your heart and mind to knowing and serving God.

> *But I fear that, as the serpent deceived Eve by his cunning, your minds may be seduced from a sincere and pure devotion to Christ. (2 Corinthians 11:3)*

Most of us know the story of Adam and Eve and the serpent. They were formed by God and placed in paradise. He gave them responsibilities, but their lives were amazing. They only had one command: don't eat from this one tree.

But the serpent placed doubts in Eve. His temptation came from questioning God:

- Did God really mean what He said?
- Is God telling you the truth?

For thousands of years, he has approached followers of God and stirred the same doubts. Even those who have sincere and pure devotion to Christ can be swayed by the serpent.

Protect your mind. Saturate it with the truth of the Bible; surround yourself with wise men and women who will guide you and turn your heart and mind to God over and over each day.

TO GO . . .

Review the story of Adam and Eve and the serpent in Genesis 3. As you go, ask God to show you an area where you doubt who He is and what He says.

Whatever is true, whatever is honorable, whatever is just, whatever is pure, whatever is lovely, whatever is commendable . . . dwell on these things. (Philippians 4:8)

Where does your mind go when you're bored? Stressed? Confused? Unsure? Planning? Praying?

You may think your mind does its own thing, taking you through memories or considering the future. But you have way more power over your mind than you realize.

The Greek word for dwell in today's verse means to consider, meditate on, determine, compute, and take account. It's a deliberate state of mind, choosing to focus.

So as you daydream, ponder, or contemplate, go through the mental checklist; does it meet the standards of Philippians 4:8? Consider asking:

- Would God lead me to these thoughts?
- Am I praising God with my mind right now?
- Is this an excellent thing to think about?
- Does this add beauty to the world?

TO GO . . .

The word translated *dwell* in today's passage is *credit* in Romans 4. See how many times you can find it. As you go, keep the Philippians 4:8 checklist handy and glance at it throughout the day.

For God has not given us a spirit of fear, but one of power, love, and sound judgment. (2 Timothy 1:7)

What are the things you shy away from? What situations make you want to run away?

That's the idea Paul is forming in today's passage. Depending on the translation you have, the word for fear above might also read timidity or cowardice. Paul is pointing out the things that make us spiritual cowards.

Have you considered your fears? Maybe you fear . . .

- confrontation.
- temptation.
- unsafe or unplanned circumstances.
- failure.

When you find yourself behaving in a timid, fearful, or cowardly way, use 2 Timothy 1:7 to tell yourself, *This is not from God.* God has made you smart, loving, and powerful. He equipped your mind to know and believe Him, trusting His will and His wisdom in every situation.

You have an amazing mind; fill it with knowledge of God, and choose to believe His promises. Then you'll be able to rely on God's power with love and sound judgment.

TO GO . . .

See what insight Isaiah 11:2 adds to today's passage. As you go, confess to God where you're timid; ask Him to make you brave.

The one who trusts in himself is a fool, but one who walks in wisdom will be safe. (Proverbs 28:26)

You are loved by God. You are amazing. You were given gifts and talents and blessings you can't even fathom.

But you shouldn't trust yourself. Seriously! If you're honest, you'll even admit it:

- You're selfish.
- You don't love others well.
- You have no idea what the future holds.
- You often make lazy, sinful, or foolish choices.

These statements are true of everyone. When we live according to our own desires, innately, we fall short of anything great.

We are all inherently sinful. So what in the world do we do? We depend on God. We trust that He alone knows what is good and best and loving. We give Him the authority to tell us truth, and we live according to His Word. We walk in His wisdom.

Find confidence in who you are, but don't trust yourself. Trust God.

TO GO . . .

Find out how else you should walk in Ephesians 5:1 and Romans 6:4. As you go, ask God to help you find your true identity and confidence in Him.

> *We demolish arguments and every proud thing*
> *that is raised up against the knowledge of God,*
> *and we take every thought captive to obey Christ.*
> *(2 Corinthians 10:4–5)*

Have you ever seen a building demolished? It's completely destroyed and every piece is hauled off. Sometimes it's dismantled piece by piece, sometimes it's imploded with explosives, sometimes it's knocked down by a wrecking ball or an excavator.

Today's passage gives us instructions on what we are to demolish in our lives: any thought that stands against the knowledge of God.

What might qualify?

- "It's not that big of a deal; everyone's doing it."
- "God doesn't really care If I _____."
- "It's my life; I can do what I want."
- "What my parents don't know won't hurt them."

These thoughts are dangerous. They set your mind and heart against the power and love of God. Demolish these ideas with the truth of the Scripture and the power of believing God. You belong to Christ; one of your responsibilities is to take ownership of every thought.

TO GO . . .

Read Paul's entire thought in 2 Corinthians 10:1–6. As you go, create an image of yourself demolishing a false belief. Blow it to bits!

*Set your minds on things above, not on earthly
things. For you died, and your life is hidden with
Christ in God. (Colossians 3:2–3)*

Look at the word *set* in today's passage. What have you "set" recently?

- Did you set the table, arranging silverware and dishes in a particular way?
- Did you set out on an adventure, ready with the proper supplies?
- Did you set a timer to end a nap or stop studying?

When you set something, you've done it intentionally with a goal in mind.

So where have you set your mind? Have you set it on the things of this world or the things beyond it?

Even though our minds are powerful, we have the potential to set them where we want them to go. Some people set their minds on earthly things: attention, looks, approval, power.

But as followers of Jesus, we set our minds on things above: the glory of God, choosing to believe His Word, showing others who He is.

TO GO . . .

Look at 1 Peter 1:13 to find something else we're called to set. As you go, picture yourself setting your mind on things above. What does that look like?

*He renews my life; he leads me along the right
paths for his name's sake. (Psalm 23:3)*

What makes a person truly alive? Is there a difference between being
scientifically alive and being aware of your passions, emotions, thoughts,
and energies?

Today's passage is from Psalm 23. The opening phrase is sometimes
translated, "He restores my soul." The word for soul is interchangeable
with *life*, which points to the essence that makes a person alive.

How does God renew our lives and restore our souls?

- He gives us new strength.
- He lets us breathe and rest.
- He invigorates our energy.
- He refreshes us spiritually and emotionally.

Your soul is what makes you feel and know you're alive. Life and hard
times and struggles can wear out your soul, but God can renew it.

What do we do with our renewed lives? We follow God. He leads us
on the right paths after supplying us with the renewal to keep going. God
opens the path; He refreshes and is glorified by our lives.

TO GO . . .

Look at what else refreshes in Romans 15:32 and
1 Corinthians 16:18. As you go, thank God for renewing
you. Praise Him for leading you.

Why, my soul, are you so dejected? Why are you in such turmoil? Put your hope in God, for I will still praise him, my Savior and my God. (Psalm 43:5)

Have you ever talked to yourself? Out loud? Some people think it's a crazy thing to do; others say it's a healthy outlet for thinking through decisions. In today's passage, the psalmist is not simply talking to himself—he's talking to his soul.

What is a soul? Consider the different parts of your body: mind, heart, body, emotions, and attitudes. Your soul is the deep-down part of all those things. Your soul is the center of your living being. It's what makes you the unique person you are.

And sometimes you need to talk to it. Why? Because sometimes our souls can become:

- frustrated
- anxious
- fearful
- depressed

So when your soul turns sour or doubtful, follow the example of the psalmist and have a good talk with it. Speak truth!

TO GO . . .

Find the two times that a psalmist speaks to his soul in Psalm 42. As you go, reflect on your soul right now. What is its condition?

93 *SOUL*

My soul, bless the Lord, and all that is within me, bless his holy name. My soul, bless the Lord, and do not forget all his benefits. (Psalm 103:1–2)

If a teacher repeats something in class, it must be important. You're wise to write it down to remember it for a test. The Bible is the same way.

If the Bible repeats something, we're wise to pay attention to it; it must be extremely important.

Notice the phrase mentioned twice in today's passage: "My soul, bless the Lord." And then it tells how:

- Bless His name with all that is within you. Consider all the potential you have to use from inside: relationships, talents, energy, enthusiasm, encouragement, passion, leadership, and joy. We bless God when all these things point to Him and reveal who He is.

- Do not forget His benefits. He loves, He blesses, He helps, He protects, He leads, and He prepares. This incomplete list is just a taste of the benefits of God.

When your soul blesses the Lord, your mind and heart focus on Him.

TO GO . . .

Read all of Psalm 103. As you go, start a list of God's benefits. Add to it for the rest of this study, each time you remember something new.

"For what does it benefit someone to gain the whole world and yet lose his life?" (Mark 8:36)

The world—the things that do not revere or acknowledge God—is a powerful force. There are people everywhere who choose to follow the world because of what it offers:

- power
- money
- temporary satisfaction
- self-sufficiency

On the surface, those things sound good, right? But consider what you give up when you choose to adhere to the teachings of the world: God as Lord and Savior. Without Him, we lose our guidance, our hope, our joy, our supernatural blessings, and our promise of eternity.

And, according to Mark 8:36, you also lose your life. That word for life is sometimes translated as *soul.* Meaning that if we choose to gain the world, we lose our identity in God, which is who we were made to be in Jesus. Gaining the world may lead to temporary success but eternal loss.

We live in the world, but the world is not our goal. Set your heart and mind on Jesus.

TO GO . . .

Read Mark 8:34–35 to see the preceding conversation. As you go, ask the Holy Spirit to show you the areas where you're seeking to gain the world.

> *But from there, you will search for the Lord your God, and you will find him when you seek him with all your heart and all your soul. (Deuteronomy 4:29)*

Think about the last time you lost something. What did you do to find it? Did you retrace your steps? Look carefully with a flashlight or even on your hands and knees? Ask others if they had seen it?

God is near and present, but He is invisible to our human eyes. Because of that, we search for Him differently than we would search for something we lost.

We search for God with our heart and our soul. In God's plan, eyes and hands and mouths don't do much good in finding Him. But He promises that we will find Him if we . . .

- tune our minds to knowing His Word and believing it.
- set our affections and passions on Him and His plan.
- praise Him with our inward and outward expressions.
- submit to His wisdom, His plan, and His glory.

TO GO . . .

Look at how Jeremiah 29:13 backs up the words in today's passage. As you go, consider how you are seeking God daily. What disciplines can you add?

This is what the L̲o̲r̲d̲ says: Stand by the roadways and look. Ask about the ancient paths, "Which is the way to what is good?" Then take it and find rest for yourselves. (Jeremiah 6:16)

Trying to figure out life seems crazy. There are so many voices telling you what to do, where to go, and what to think.

But there is comfort and promise in today's Scripture:

- There are good paths.
- They are ancient.
- You can find them if you ask and look.

Don't be afraid to view your life as a long journey. There are other travelers, dangerous turns, unlabeled forks, and tricky terrain. You've never been there before, but others have.

So ask them! Cultivate friendships with people of different generations and inquire, "What did you do in this situation?" "What Scriptures might help me here?" "Would you pray for me?"

Finding the ancient, good paths lead to rest for your soul. Even though you're on a journey, you can have peace.

TO GO . . .

See what else brings rest to your soul in Psalm 62:5 and Psalm 116:7. As you go, decide on one person whose wisdom you need in your life. Contact him or her today.

97 *SOUL*

Dear friend, I pray that you are prospering in every way and are in good health, just as your whole life is going well. (3 John 2)

You know that, as followers of Jesus, we are called to pray for others in good times and bad. Sometimes we struggle to know how to pray for others. Today's passage gives us some guidance. It comes from a letter the apostle John wrote to a friend.

He speaks of two things in the friend's life:

- good health (physical well-being)
- life going well (spiritual well-being)

As is often the case in Scripture, the word for life can also be translated *soul*. So as John is praying that his friend's body is healthy, he is praying that his soul is healthy, as well.

Think about what having a cold or injury does: it affects your mood, your appetite. It makes you grumpy, tired, and miserable. In the same way, spiritual sickness can affect every aspect of your life.

TO GO . . .

Find several other things to pray for others in Ephesians 1:17–19. As you go, pray for your sick friends; not just for physical healing but for soul wellness.

"Now my soul is troubled. What should I say—
Father, save me from this hour? But that is why I
came to this hour." (John 12:27)

Jesus experienced all that we experience: friendship, joy, and fun. He also went through trials, sadness, and sorrow. Today's passage is a quote from Jesus near the time of His crucifixion.

Even though Jesus had full confidence in God's plan and was certain that He was called to this very purpose, His soul was troubled. That phrase "is troubled" could also be translated:

- in turmoil
- deeply distressed
- heartbroken
- storm tossed
- torn within

Have you ever felt this way? Jesus did too. His example gives us the freedom to struggle, to cry out, and to pray to God honestly. Jesus understands. He's been there. He can help!

But notice that Jesus didn't pray to miss the trial; He was confident that the trial was part of God's plan for Him. Your trials are part of your life path, as well.

TO GO . . .

Read about the entire scene in John 12:20–36. As you go, recall a time when your soul was troubled. Thank God for His help in that time.

Though you have not seen him, you love him;
though not seeing him now, you believe in him,
and you rejoice with inexpressible and glorious
joy. (1 Peter 1:8)

Years after Jesus' death and resurrection, Peter wrote to some of Jesus' followers far away; today's passage comes from that letter. In his opening words, Peter praised God, spoke truth, and gave hope to those men and women.

Peter was also excited by their faith! Though they had never seen Jesus personally, they . . .

- loved Him.
- believed in Him.
- rejoiced.

Sometimes, it feels like it would have been easier to follow Jesus if we'd lived at the time that He lived. You might think, "If Jesus were here in the flesh, I would have no problem believing Him." Maybe so, but your trust would be based on what you see, not what you believe!

True faith—faith without seeing—is what brings us to salvation.

TO GO . . .

Read the opening of Peter's letter in 1 Peter 1:1–9. As you go, thank God for the ability to believe and love Jesus without seeing Him.

We have this hope as an anchor for the soul, firm and secure. (Hebrews 6:19)

The book of Hebrews points back to many Old Testament stories and shows how we can learn about faith and hope through those men and women who loved and obeyed God even before Jesus came to earth as a baby.

Today's verse is pointing back to the promise God made to Abraham—that He would bless Abraham and multiply his family. It took many years for Abraham to see the promise that God made actually happen; however, as he waited, he confidently trusted in God's promise.

Like Abraham, you can fix your soul to the hope of God's promises. Like an anchor in rough, stormy seas, you can use His promises to give you stability and comfort during the storms of life.

These are just some of His promises:

- He loves you.
- He is with you always.
- He will never leave you.
- He will save you.

TO GO . . .

Read more about God's promise to Abraham in Genesis 12:1–3. As you go, draw an anchor on your wrist. Use it to remind you to have hope in God's promises.

101

Now in this hope we were saved, but hope that is seen is not hope, because who hopes for what he sees? Now if we hope for what we do not see, we eagerly wait for it with patience. (Romans 8:24–25)

How have you used the word *hope* lately?

- "I hope she forgets to give us that quiz."
- "I hope I get at least a B on that paper."
- "I hope I don't run out of gas before I get home."

We hope for many things, but our daily hopes are another way of expressing what we want to happen.

The hope that we have through faith in Jesus is different; it's based in Him. We hope for eternity; we hope for peace, for guidance, and we hope for unfailing love . . . not simply because it's what we want but because it's what Jesus tells us we can have.

There's just one issue; there's no physical, visual guarantee. You can't see the promise of His hope, but you can know it's there.

TO GO . . .

Read Hebrews 11:1 to see what hope and faith have in common. As you go, consider one thing you are hoping for in Jesus. Say it out loud as you pray.

You will be confident, because there is hope. You will look carefully about and lie down in safety. (Job 11:18)

Poor Job had lost everything: possessions, children, health, and even respect. He was struggling with why God had allowed all this to happen. His well-meaning friends tried giving him some advice: repent because you must have sinned. The problem was that Job hadn't sinned. Their advice was not grounded in God's sovereignty.

There is, however, truth in what Job's friend Zophar said to him in today's passage: when you turn your heart to God (Job 11:18), you can have confidence because there is hope in Him. We often try to find confidence in ourselves, our strengths, our situation, or even our hard work, but the only lasting, solid confidence comes from our hope in God.

Our hope in God gives us confidence in:

- salvation
- eternity
- being loved
- forgiveness
- God's presence

We find God's confidence when we base our hope fully on God.

TO GO . . .

Read Zophar's words to Job in the entire chapter of Job 11. As you go, consider this statement: "I can be confident in _____ because I hope in the Lord."

*Be strong, and let your heart be courageous, all
you who put your hope in the L*ORD*. (Psalm 31:24)*

You're probably hoping for something; but where are you putting your hope?

- Is your hope in good luck, knowing there's a chance something could happen?
- Is your hope in other people, believing they will come through for you?
- Is your hope in your own abilities, sure that you can make something happen?

When we put our hope in luck, others, or even ourselves, there's a good chance we will be disappointed.

But putting our hope in the Lord is different. Why? It's because He is the only one that is totally dependable. Our hope should be based in Him because He is all knowing, all powerful, and full of love.

When your hope is in God, you walk and believe in His strength, which makes you truly strong. You can be courageous because He is perfectly able to protect you. His strength and power enable you to have strength and courage.

TO GO . . .

See what else you can learn about gaining a courageous heart in Psalm 27:14. As you go, picture what a courageous heart looks like in cartoon form. Maybe even sketch it.

> *"For I know the plans I have for you"—this is the*
> *LORD's declaration—"plans for your well-being,*
> *not for disaster, to give you a future and a hope."*
> *(Jeremiah 29:11)*

This verse is one people love to quote when times are good. It's actually a pretty tough one to believe when you're struggling.

Jeremiah was delivering today's passage to the Israelites just after giving them some terrible news: they were going to be exiled for seventy years!

Like the Israelites, you've probably gotten some bad news too:

- The person you love is not going to get well.
- Your friend is moving away.
- Your family is breaking apart.
- What you had planned for the future can't happen.

It's times like these when we question if God loves us, if He cares, or if He even sees us. Jeremiah reminds us that God has a plan that is for our well-being, and He has our future and hope in mind. We can be confident that God's plan—whether good or bad—gives us a future and a hope in Him.

TO GO . . .

Read this part of Jeremiah's letter in Jeremiah 29:1–14. As you go, consider one area of your life that seems out of control. Tell God you trust His plan.

> *I will praise you forever for what you have done. In the presence of your faithful people, I will put my hope in your name, for it is good. (Psalm 52:9)*

As soon as God brought the Israelites out of slavery in Egypt, He began to reveal His plan for a tabernacle. It would be a place where the presence of God would dwell and where His people would gather to worship. God had a plan for His people to be together and worship Him.

He plans the same thing for us today. We are blessed when we're around other believers regularly. Each church is a little different, but almost all of them:

- pray
- study the Bible
- sing praises
- speak words of faith
- share their stories

In today's passage, David adds another element of congregational gatherings: putting our hope in God's name. When you share what He has done in your life and who you know Him to be, you declare you have confident faith in Him.

TO GO . . .

Find out more about the "faithful people" of a congregation in 2 Chronicles 6:41 and Psalm 132:16. As you go, make a mental list of three things God has done for you recently.

*I have a hope in God, which these men themselves
also accept, that there will be a resurrection, both
of the righteous and the unrighteous. (Acts 24:15)*

Today's passage contains the words of Paul, who was standing on trial
before the governor. The Jews had grown angry at Paul because of His
belief in Jesus and were actually trying to have him killed. After the
Jewish leaders had brought their case against him, Paul explained that he
had done nothing to deserve death.

Paul summed up his faith like this:

- He worshiped and believed God (Acts 24:14).
- He hoped in God (Acts 24:15).
- He tried to have a clear conscience toward God and men (Acts 24:16).

Following God and explaining your faith to someone doesn't have to
be complicated or confusing. Your hope in God may be upsetting, offen-
sive, or even combative to people who do not share your hope; share it
anyway. Your testimony may reach even the mind and heart of a person
who despises you.

TO GO . . .

Read Daniel 6:1–10 and consider how Daniel's testimony is similar to Paul's. As you go, write out a
three-sentence statement of your own faith. Be pre-
pared to share it.

> *I wait for the LORD; I wait and put my hope in his word. (Psalm 130:5)*

Hope is a good thing to have as a believer:

- It keeps us focused on God and His plan.
- It encourages us.
- It becomes our testimony.

But there is also an element to hope that few people enjoy: waiting.

In today's passage, you see the word *wait* twice. On top of that, the word *hope* can be translated as "to wait for." Inherent in the definition of hoping is waiting. So we might even say that today's passage loosely says, "In God's word I wait and wait and wait."

Waiting doesn't come naturally or even with joy, but waiting often builds strength. A flower grows quickly but is delicate and weak. An oak tree, however, is made strong and dependable because of its slow growth. Faith that waits has the strength of an oak tree. The slow growth of God's Word in us strengthens us as we wait for it.

TO GO . . .

Read all of Psalm 130 and underline the words *hope* and *wait* each time they appear. As you go, ask God to give you stronger faith as you wait for His Word to come alive in you.

*Because of the L*ORD*'s faithful love we do not perish, for his mercies never end. They are new every morning; great is your faithfulness! I say, "The L*ORD *is my portion." (Lamentations 3:22–24)*

When a person dies, they sometimes leave an inheritance to their family. An inheritance can be a sentimental item worth no money; sometimes, it can have immense value.

The word *portion* used in today's passage is a Hebrew word that describes an inheritance. Jeremiah is considering just some of the characteristics of God:

- faithful love
- never-ending mercy
- great faithfulness

These benefits of God are our inheritance. As His children, we can be confident that they are ours to receive and keep.

Like Jeremiah, who wrote the book of Lamentations, this type of inheritance should give you great hope: you've been promised the love, mercy, and faithfulness of Almighty God.

TO GO . . .

Find out more about the Lord being your portion in Psalm 16:5 and Psalm 142:5. As you go, consider all the things promised to you as God's child. Add to the list above.

> *May your faithful love rest on us, Lord, for we put*
> *our hope in you. (Psalm 33:22)*

One of the greatest joys in life is wrapping yourself up in a fuzzy blanket on a cold morning. Even better, maybe, is pulling a steaming hot blanket out of the dryer and wrapping it around you. There's nothing quite like being wrapped in warmth in the middle of the cold.

Did you know that God's mercy—His faithful, steadfast, covenant love—does the same thing? It gives comfort, peace, joy, and confidence even in the most difficult days.

In today's passage, the psalmist reveals what happens when we put our hope in the Lord: His faithful love rests on us. His love . . .

- is upon us.
- is over us.
- is with us.
- surrounds us.
- overshadows us.
- drenches us.

We can know and believe and feel God's mercy all around us like a warm blanket. Put your hope in the Lord, and wait in expectation for His mercy.

TO GO . . .

Observe how Psalm 62:5 adds to your understanding of Psalm 33:22. As you go, wrap a jacket or scarf around you. Let it remind you of God's merciful love.

We have also obtained access through him by faith into this grace in which we stand, and we rejoice in the hope of the glory of God. (Romans 5:2)

Have you ever stood in a puddle? Even better, have you ever watched a small child stand in one? Puddles have been known to bring joy to kids as their shoes and socks get soaked.

According to today's passage, we can stand in grace just like a child stands in a puddle: rejoicing. But instead of getting soaked in water, we get soaked in hope!

Specifically, we can hope in the glory of God. That means we have confident faith that God will be revealed: through His creation, through His children (us!), through His Word, or through His mighty works.

Romans 5:2 is not a long verse, but it contains so much truth. Let's break it into bite-sized chunks:

- We stand in grace.
- Grace comes through faith.
- We hope in the glory of God.
- Hope in God's glory leads us to rejoice.

TO GO . . .

See what you can learn about standing in grace in 1 Peter 5:12. As you go, stand in a puddle, in the sun, or in the rain, and dwell on the idea of standing in grace.

> *"I do not call you servants anymore, because a servant doesn't know what his master is doing. I have called you friends." (John 15:15)*

How would you identify yourself? Young, smart, energetic, creative, bold?

How might others identify you? Sassy, loving, helpful, quiet, imaginative?

Your identity can come from many aspects and opinions. Any human description, however, is temporary: based on mood, health, time, or mind-set.

Identity found in God, however, is eternal. When God declares your identity, it can't be changed. And in today's passage, Jesus shares one aspect of who His followers are: His friends.

Even though the message was originally spoken to His disciples, it applies to us, as well. Like them, you started out as a listener or learner of Jesus; as you know Him, trust Him, and truly walk in His footsteps, you also become a friend. That friendship is not just lifelong; it's eternal!

TO GO . . .

Dig deeper into what Jesus taught about being His friend in John 15:13–14. As you go, ponder this question: what does it mean to be Jesus' friend?

*Don't make friends with an angry person, and
don't be a companion of a hot-tempered one, or
you will learn his ways and entangle yourself in a
snare. (Proverbs 22:24–25)*

The Bible has quite a lot to say about friendship. Much of that advice is about who shouldn't be your friend.

Today's passage instructs you not to make friends with an angry or hot-tempered person. Why?

- You'll learn his (or her!) ways.
- You'll entangle yourself in a snare.

This verse doesn't imply that your friends must never get angry, but it does imply that anger does not mark their lives and that anger does not overcome them in hard situations.

Following God doesn't mean that we ignore the things that make us angry, but it does mean that we choose to trust, worship, wait on, and praise God even in the midst of them. We also choose to love and forgive others even when we're angry.

If anger overtakes our ability to obey and believe God, it will rule over us.

TO GO . . .

Learn more about anger in Ephesians 4:26–27. As you go, ask God if your anger is out of control. Ask a mentor to help you start working through it.

Do not be deceived: "Bad company corrupts good morals." (1 Corinthians 15:33)

Whether we realize it or not, every person we count as a friend influences us. When you were little, your friends probably showed you a cool new way to tie your shoes or convinced you to like a particular game. As you get older, your friends open your mind to new ideas, attitudes, or interests.

Sometimes our friends are positive, godly influences. Sometimes they lead us away from God and toward sin.

"Not me," you say. "I can be around people who aren't good influences and they don't affect me." Wrong. This is exactly why Paul began this verse with, "Do not be deceived."

Friends that draw you closer to God will . . .

- show you mercy, grace, and love.
- help you live an honorable, honest life.
- point you to God in struggles.
- speak truth and wisdom.

Your friends don't have to be perfect, but, at the same time, don't just settle for friends who drag you down.

TO GO . . .

Look at another warning against being deceived in James 1:13–18. As you go, commit some time tonight to praying over your friends. Ask God where you're being corrupted and how to handle that relationship.

But Elisha replied, "As the LORD lives and as you yourself live, I will not leave you." (2 Kings 2:2)

There are several biblical examples of great friendship. Today's passage points to another pair you might not have heard of: Elisha and Elijah.

- Elijah had been a mighty prophet in Israel during the days of King Ahab. He stood against idolatry and showed God's people what it meant to follow Him. God worked in powerful ways through him: Elijah called fire from heaven, raised a boy from the dead, and outran a chariot.

- Elisha was a farmer who was called by Elijah to follow him in being God's prophet. Elisha committed to learning from Elijah and became God's spokesman after Elijah was carried to heaven in a chariot of fire.

These men had different personalities, different strengths, and were from different generations. But both loved God, strengthened each other with their faith, and changed the hearts of the people around them. They were committed to God as well as to each other. That's true friendship!

TO GO . . .

Read more about Elijah (1 Kings 18:20–46) and Elisha (2 Kings 2). As you go, ask God to point you to a godly friendship you need to invest in.

> *Now when Job's three friends . . . heard about all this adversity that had happened to him, each of them came from his home. They met together to go and sympathize with him and comfort him. (Job 2:11)*

Sometimes we have friends go through incredibly hard times:

- death of a loved one
- lasting sickness or illness
- family tragedy
- abuse or neglect
- personal or community violence

Even though we know we should help or at least talk to them, many people avoid their struggling friends because they don't know what to do or say. Some think it's just too awkward; others might be afraid of making them feel worse.

Consider what Job's friends did after he had suffered immense loss: they went to him, sympathized with him, and comforted him.

We would be wise to do the same when our friends are in need. Be available for your friend. Bring comfort into his life. Share your own struggles, and encourage them to place their hope in God.

TO GO . . .

Don't forget that God is our greatest comforter. Look in Psalm 23:4, 71:21, and 94:19. As you go, commit to never avoiding friends who are struggling. Be a source of comfort and support.

The one who walks with the wise will become
wise, but a companion of fools will suffer harm.
(Proverbs 13:20)

Wisdom is not just for adults. You may be a teenager, but you are more than ready to possess and use wisdom.

According to the Bible, and the book of Proverbs specifically, foolishness is the opposite of wisdom, and wisdom can't be reached by surrounding yourself with fools.

What are some characteristics of fools?

- disregarding God's identity and authority
- treating others with no love or compassion or respect
- ignoring moral standards, laws, and common sense
- pretending cruelty and harm is entertaining

There's a pretty good chance that one or more of your friends come to mind as you read this list. There's a pretty good chance that the more time you spend with that person, the more likely it is that you're doing foolish things or becoming foolish in general.

You are not too young to surround yourself with wise friends. They aren't common, but they exist! Find wise people and invest in those relationships.

TO GO . . .

Read more about God's definition of wisdom in Proverbs 2. As you go, choose to pray for and love your foolish friends, but minimize your time with them.

Put on compassion, kindness, humility, gentleness, and patience, bearing with one another and forgiving one another if anyone has a grievance against one another. (Colossians 3:12–13)

Are you a list-maker? Do you start your day or study session with a good list? There's a joy that comes from marking off that last item.

Believe it or not; Paul was a list-maker. Throughout his letters (the books of Romans through Philemon), you'll find many places where Paul made lists. Today's passage is one of them.

This particular list could be entitled, "How to be a good friend." It starts with knowing that you belong to God, believing you have been made holy and are loved by Him. Because of that, you choose to be . . .

- compassionate.
- kind.
- humble.
- gentle.
- patient.
- loyal.
- forgiving.

This is not an easy list, but if you keep this list in your heart and your mind, you'll practice the skills necessary to be a great friend.

TO GO . . .

Look at another list close to today's passage in Colossians 3:5–10. As you go, consider writing these items on a to-do list.

The wounds of a friend are trustworthy, but the kisses of an enemy are excessive. (Proverbs 27:6)

Few things are more dangerous than a friend who makes everything seem okay. We're all flawed. We're born selfish, prideful, and sinful. We don't know everything, but we often pretend we do. We make choices that don't glorify God or lead us down His path for our lives. So it is not in your best interest to have someone in your life who says, "It's no big deal!" "Do what you want!"

A real friend—a friend who points you to Jesus—will honestly tell you:

- "This is a bad idea."
- "You're out of God's plan here."
- "This goes against the Bible."
- "I'm not going to let you make this mistake."

You may not like what they say, and it might even make you upset for a minute, but if you're genuinely seeking God, you'll consider their words. After all, truth that hurts is still truth. Friends who keep you from your own sin are the real ones.

TO GO . . .

Find out more about trustworthy people in Proverbs 11:13 and 13:17. As you go, make a mental list of friends who would give you trustworthy words. Thank God for them.

Two are better than one because they have a good reward for their efforts. For if either falls, his companion can lift him up; but pity the one who falls without another to lift him up. (Ecclesiastes 4:9–10)

Fair-weather friends are always there when life is fun, times are good, and everybody is happy. They're kind when you're kind, helpful when you're helpful, forgiving when you're forgiving.

But real friends go beyond:

- They are still around when we go through storms, heartbreak, and trials.
- They give grace when we lose patience, understanding the situation and our struggles.
- They help us see God's hand, believe God's Word, and identify God's glory.

Some people use this passage as a way to measure their friends; however, an even better use is as a tool to check yourself. Are you there for your friends when they struggle? Do you show compassion and empathy? Can you love them through the tough times?

Lift up your friends; be their helper and lifter.

TO GO . . .

Read Ecclesiastes 4:4–16 to set this verse in context. As you go, pray that God will show you how to lift up a friend who has fallen or who is struggling.

*Iron sharpens iron, and one person sharpens
another. (Proverbs 27:17)*

When Solomon wrote the verse in today's passage, iron was the latest
and greatest technology. Civilizations had just exited the Bronze Age, in
which they used stone and bronze as their primary materials for making
tools. Discovering iron changed everything because it made their tools
stronger and longer lasting; we still use iron today.

Iron was so strong, though, that it took more iron to make it sharp. You
couldn't sharpen your gardening tools with a rock or wood; you needed
more iron.

Similarly, people change each other, but not always for the better:

- Some people make others bitter, only bringing anger and
  jealousy.
- Some people make others lazy, allowing selfish desires to overcome responsibility.
- Some people, however, can make others better with encouragement and support.

We are wise to look at our friendships and ask, *How is this sharpening
me? Am I growing closer to wisdom and love and Jesus or am I becoming
less of who He created me to be?*

TO GO . . .

See what else you can learn about iron in Isaiah 48:4
and Jeremiah 15:12. As you go, answer this question
honestly: how do you sharpen others?

121 PRAYER

> *"Whenever you pray, say, 'Father, your name be honored as holy. . . . Give us each day our daily bread.'" (Luke 11:2–3)*

"Lord, teach us to pray." That was the request of one of Jesus' disciples. Not surprisingly, the request was made just after Jesus was "praying in a certain place" (Luke 11:1).

What made the disciple ask for help? Maybe it's because he had the same struggles we have with prayer today:

- difficulty knowing what to pray
- struggle to stay focused on God
- unable to pray without selfishness or pride
- being disciplined enough to pray at all

In order to help, Jesus gave a model prayer. It started with giving attention and honor to God. When the prayer turned to the person praying, the request was simply "daily bread," or just enough to survive.

We would be wise to follow the same example. Before asking a single thing of God, focus on Him. Remember who He is and what He has done. Let His holiness and identity guide your prayer. Then trust Him to get you through today.

TO GO . . .

Read the entire prayer in Luke 11:1–4. Then read verses 5–13 too. As you go, make it your new habit to start your prayer by giving attention to God.

In the same way the Spirit also helps us in our weakness, because we do not know what to pray for as we should, but the Spirit himself intercedes for us with unspoken groanings. (Romans 8:26)

Many Christians feel guilty that they don't "pray like they should." Today's passage gives insight and freedom into a few reasons why:

- We are weak.
- We don't know what to pray for.

That's why we need the Spirit. When we are weak, He helps. When we don't know what to pray for, He leads us toward God's will. Sounds amazing, doesn't it? So how do we get that help from the Spirit?

Quite basically, those who live by the Spirit have access to the Spirit for their prayers. That means we read the Bible and deal with the ups and downs of life with our focus on God. Living in the Spirit means we obey God's Word and choose to believe what we know of God.

The same Spirit that lives in us through faith also guides us in prayer.

TO GO . . .

Read more about the Holy Spirit in Romans 8:26. As you go, picture the Spirit right beside you as you pray. Know and believe He is helping you.

> *Hear the petitions of your servant and your people Israel, which they pray toward this place. May you hear in your dwelling place in heaven. May you hear and forgive. (2 Chronicles 6:21)*

Today's passage comes from the mouth of King Solomon as he was dedicating the Lord's temple after he finished building it. Understanding that this would be the dwelling of the presence of God, Solomon approached its completion with honor and reverence.

Notice that he asked for God to *hear* the prayers prayed toward that temple; not once or twice, but three times he said the word *hear*.

God is never too busy or ignoring us or unaware of our needs; so why the triple request of God to hear?

The Hebrew word translated "hear" means:

- to hear or listen
- to understand
- to hear with attention or interest

Solomon was asking for God to hear and act; he was calling upon God's power. Like Solomon, we can pray knowing that God alone has the power to act. We make our requests but give Him authority.

TO GO . . .

Read this entire amazing prayer in 2 Chronicles 6.
As you go, consider whether you're talking to God or talking with God. (Big difference!)

*During those days he went out to the mountain
to pray and spent all night in prayer to God. (Luke
6:12)*

Today's passage takes place early in Jesus' earthly ministry. Even though
He had several years and many struggles to come, He had already begun
to encounter trials:

- He and His disciples were accused of breaking Jewish laws.
- He was chastised for healing on the Sabbath.
- He made the big decision of choosing His disciples.

So Jesus, knowing what had come and what would happen in the
near future, spent all night praying to God on a mountain.

There are times when we need to do the same. When you are
overwhelmed, when pressure is too much, or when a difficult time is
approaching, you need to reach out to God. With your Bible open, spend
all day or all night pouring over His Word and submitting to His authority.
More than simply telling God what you're facing, extended times of prayer
help you to depend on His promises and believe He is who He says He is.

TO GO . . .

Look at what happened after Jesus' all-night prayer in
Luke 6:12–19. As you go, commit your current difficul-
ties and challenges to God; spend time in prayer.

> *I never stop giving thanks for you as I remember
> you in my prayers. (Ephesians 1:16)*

There are many people who make a difference in your life. Whether you love them completely or wish they would move across the country, God placed them in your life for a reason. He plans to use your relationship with them to shape you and give you an opportunity to glorify Him.

Some of those relationships include:

- family, both near and extended
- school faculty
- friends and acquaintances
- younger people in your life who look up to you
- older people in your life, given as an example

The best way to know your purpose in these relationships is to remember these people—by name—in your prayers. Pray for their physical and spiritual health. Pray for the good and bad in their lives. Pray for how you can love, help, and encourage them. And after you've shared all you can think of with God, thank Him for their strengths, weaknesses, and purpose.

TO GO . . .

Find out how to pray for influential people in Ephesians 1:15–19. As you go, say out loud the names of those important people. Thank God for them.

Answer me when I call, God, who vindicates me.
You freed me from affliction; be gracious to me
and hear my prayer. (Psalm 4:1)

Many believers have the wrong idea about prayer. Many times we think of someone kneeling, praying through every person they know (or don't know but know about!) and asking God to handle situations in a particular way.

That's not prayer; that's talking to a genie. God doesn't solve problems the way we want Him to just because we pray. So let go of thinking, "This turned into a mess because I didn't pray for it!"

Prayer is one of the most important aspects of being a Christian. We're commanded, encouraged, and given examples of prayer.

Here are some of the different aspects of prayer in today's Scripture:

- seeking God's attention ("Please answer me when I call.")
- remembering who He is ("God who vindicates me.")
- remembering what He has done ("You freed me from affliction.")
- requesting things that are in His will ("Be gracious to me.")

TO GO . . .

Look up more requests of always being in God's will in Psalms 4:6 and 5:8. As you go, make Psalm 4:1 your model for your prayers for the rest of the day, using your own words.

> *"You will call to me and come and pray to me,
> and I will listen to you. You will seek me and find
> me when you search for me with all your heart."*
> *(Jeremiah 29:12–13)*

The setting of today's passage is not a pretty one. Through Jeremiah, God spoke to His people as they were being overtaken by their enemies.

Even though God was letting them suffer for their sin, He didn't erase their hope. He would still be their God. They would still be His people. And even though they had turned their back on Him, He would not turn His back on them.

Most important, He was still available to them:

- They would call and He would answer.
- They would seek Him and He would be found.

No matter how far you feel from God right now, the same holds true for you. You can reach Him through your prayer. He listens, and when we seek Him, we find Him.

TO GO . . .

Read Jeremiah 29:14, and notice the rest of the promises God made to His rebellious people. As you go, practice calling out to God. Aloud or silently, tell Him where you're struggling.

"Stay awake and pray, so that you won't enter into temptation. The spirit is willing, but the flesh is weak." (Matthew 26:41)

Jesus knew what was coming when He said this to His best friends; within a matter of hours, He would be arrested, unfairly tried, beaten, and nailed to a cross.

The disciples, however, had no clue just how dangerous and imminent the danger was.

Sometimes we treat our prayer time like Jesus' disciples did.

- We don't treat it with respect.
- We don't realize just how desperately we need it.
- We let other things keep us unfocused.
- We don't understand the circumstances we're about to face.

God knows what's coming, and He has instructed us to pray. We need Him; He is there. As our spirit enters into communication with God Almighty, He fills us with the strength, power, and hope to face even the things we don't see or understand.

Be alert, awake, and aware during your prayer time. Like Jesus, use it to prepare for the unknown of today and tomorrow.

TO GO . . .

Read the entire scene in Matthew 26:36–46. As you go, spend some free time today asking God to show you what to pray in your prayers.

May my prayer be set before you as incense,
the raising of my hands as the evening offering.
(Psalm 141:2)

Burning incense is one of the oldest and most reverent acts in the Old Testament:

- In God's first description of the temple, He included specifics for the incense altar and details on how the high priest should light it. Along with sacrifices, it was a daily part of worship.

- Incense was made from a variety of spices and substances which, when lit, not only had a strong smell but also a visible smoke. The smoke reminded God's people that their prayers rose to heaven.

Few churches today light incense as part of worship, but we would be wise to recall the imagery of incense as we pray. We may not understand it, but prayer is the pathway between us and God, made possible by the Holy Spirit.

Like the ancient Israelites, our time of prayer is still part of our lifestyle of worship and sacrifice. Set apart this holy time throughout the day.

TO GO . . .

Read more about incense in the temple in Exodus 30. As you go, picture a visible connection between you and God as you pray to Him today.

*The L*ORD *is near all who call out to him, all who call out to him with integrity. (Psalm 145:18)*

Today's passage is a comforting verse. It reminds us that God is near those who call out to him "with integrity." That phrase can also mean "in truth," "without guile," or "sincerely."

How can we know that we're praying to Him with integrity?

- Do you come to God believing He is almighty and all-knowing? Do you depend fully on Him to answer?
- Is He your source of wisdom, hope, and confidence?
- Does your prayer honor Him, bring Him glory, and reflect His identity according to the Bible?
- Are you being honest with God, with others, and with yourself about your situation?

Imagine Jesus sitting beside you as you pray, taking in every word. He loves you, He hears you, and He sees all that's going on with you. When you look back at Him, confess your sins, commit your situation to Him, and depend on Him to act on your behalf.

TO GO . . .

Discover who else the Lord is near in Psalm 34:18. As you go, call out to God today with integrity. Check your heart every time you pray.

> *"Honor your father and your mother so that you may have a long life in the land that the Lord your God is giving you." (Exodus 20:12)*

Today's passage comes from God, Himself, as He proclaimed to Moses "The Ten Commandments." Jews and Christians still hold these as the foundation of all other standards for life.

Does it ever bother you that God's holy list includes honoring your father and mother? Consider just a few aspects of this command:

- The original Hebrew word translated *honor* has a basic meaning of making something heavy. Basically, it means that your parents carry weight in your life.

- This command was not given to children or teens alone, but to all of God's followers. You never outgrow this command.

- This passage is followed by the promise of a long life in the promised land; God Himself assures blessing when we obey this command.

It's more than just honoring your parents; you honor God Himself when you obey your parents.

TO GO . . .

Read all the Ten Commandments in Exodus 20:1–17. As you go, ask the Lord to reveal to you how you can honor your parents today.

Sons are indeed a heritage from the L<small>ORD</small>,
offspring, a reward. Like arrows in the hand of a
warrior are the sons born in one's youth. (Psalm
127:3–5)

Imagine being a warrior in Old Testament times. Ready for battle, you grab a bow and arrows. With these, you're confident and brave.

You are like an arrow for your parents! What does that mean?

- You help them in the challenges of life.
- You're on their side in conflicts.
- You're available to protect and provide for them.
- You represent them.

Just as God intended for the earth and creation to praise Him, He intended for each family to give Him glory, as well. Part of that plan included you—as an offspring—to be a mighty weapon for your parents.

You are part of God's blessing to your parents. From your personality to your brain to your skills and hard work, you give them peace and hope.

TO GO . . .

Look at some other imagery using arrows in Psalm 144:6 and Proverbs 25:18. As you go, make up your mind to be a reward to your parents. What can you do for them today?

> *But from eternity to eternity the Lord's faithful love is toward those who fear him, and his righteousness toward the grandchildren of those who keep his covenant. (Psalm 103:17–18)*

God's faithful love does not last just one lifetime. Think about it: if you know and love God, your life reveals that:

- You talk about Him.
- You give your cares to Him.
- You trust Him for your future.

Your family sees it, your friends see it, and there's a good chance that even strangers see it.

This is the reasoning behind today's passage. It's not that one person's salvation drips down to his or her grandchildren (it doesn't), but those who witness God's faithful love in your life are impacted by your faith.

Look down the road; what will your children and grandchildren remember about your faith? Be intentional in observing God's precepts. People whose lives have pointed to Jesus have impacted your faith; as you walk in faithfulness, your life will too.

TO GO . . .

Read more about God's generational impact in Deuteronomy 7:9. As you go, thank God for the people in your life who have shown you what it means to follow God.

FAMILY **134**

He was a devout man and feared God along with
his whole household. He did many charitable
deeds for the Jewish people and always prayed to
God. (Acts 10:2)

Today's passage is about a man named Cornelius, a Roman centurion. Romans were not traditionally known for their faith in the one true God, but obviously, someone had pointed this Roman warrior to the God of Abraham and he believed.

Look at the descriptions of Cornelius in today's passage:

- devout (pious, godly) man
- feared God
- did charitable deeds
- always prayed

We can only speculate how Cornelius would stand out in our communities and churches today; just imagine how he stood out among the rough world of ancient Rome, particularly among the military men he commanded. A truly prayerful life cannot only exist privately; constant communication with God spreads into how we follow God and interact with others, as well.

God blessed Cornelius's entire family because of his obedient faith. How is your faith impacting your family?

TO GO . . .

Read the whole story by reading all of Acts 10. As you go, rededicate your prayer life to God. Is your faith a characteristic that others notice?

> The one who profits dishonestly troubles his
> household, but the one who hates bribes will live.
> (Proverbs 15:27)

"I wish my mom wouldn't get so upset about it. It's not hurting anybody."

Perhaps you know someone involved in drugs or alcohol, an inappropriate relationship, or even a crime of some sort. Sometimes, they will seem very offended that a parent or another adult is trying to steer them away from this behavior; they think they're not affecting others.

This is not true. One person's sin can impact his or her family's . . .

- finances.
- reputation.
- peace.
- focus.
- faith.

God placed you in a family. Even though you exist as individuals, you function together as a unit. One person's issues—attitude, stress level, health, focus, patience, love, and time—affect the unit as a whole.

Wise believers understand that their lives are interconnected; love for family and love for God work hand in hand. You honor your family best when you live according to God's standards.

TO GO . . .

Read more about the righteous and the wicked in Proverbs 11. As you go, ask God to reveal to you how you impact your family, for better or worse.

*As for me and my family, we will worship the Lᴏʀᴅ.
(Joshua 24:15)*

No two families are the same, and the things that make your family unique are the things you do together. Maybe you go to the beach or read novels. Perhaps your family has a game night or goes to sporting events.

One of the most beneficial things a family can do, though, is worship the Lord. Remember that worshiping includes singing and praising at church, but it also involves a lifestyle of honor, thanksgiving, and obedience to God.

So what might worship look like as a family?

- singing praise songs as you ride in the car
- talking about what you're learning from the Bible
- praying for friends and family who need to believe God
- encouraging each other with truth from God's Word

You might be the only one in your family who worships God; maybe doing some of these things with them can help them see your faith. Your lifestyle of worship could even change their hearts.

TO GO . . .

Read this powerful speech from Israel's leader in Joshua 24:1–28. As you go, consider one way you can worship with your family this week.

My son, keep your father's command, and don't reject your mother's teaching. (Proverbs 6:20)

The book of Proverbs was written by King Solomon and intended for his son. Many of the statements in the book address his son directly.

On top of that, remember that Solomon was the wisest person in Scripture, made wise by God Himself. So when you read the words of Proverbs, picture an all-powerful king, wise beyond comprehension, looking you in the eyes and telling you things for your good.

Today's message: honor and obey your parents.

This is a struggle for almost every teen at one point or another. Why? Teens should be growing in wisdom and responsibility as parents choose to relinquish some of their control. However, this plan doesn't always happen due to rebellion, foolishness, scorn, sin, or misunderstanding.

Teens aren't always to blame for harsh relationships with their parents; adults are sinful and human too. Your command to honor your parents, however, is non-negotiable. It's wise and good to obey your parents.

TO GO . . .

Read more about Solomon's wisdom for his son in Proverbs 6:21–23. As you go, choose to change any rebellious or foolish attitudes toward your parents.

Children, obey your parents in everything, for this pleases the Lord. (Colossians 3:20)

Parents are to protect, teach, love, and help their children so that they will grow well. Most parents have the best of intentions for their children and give them standards and rules for their best. Still, most children ask, "Why do I have to do that?"

The reasons are many:

- Your parents have authority over you.
- They love you.
- They are responsible for you.
- They are older, wiser, and have an understanding you don't.

But today's passage points to another reason that children (and teens!) are instructed to obey their parents in everything: it pleases the Lord.

Don't be misled: God knows your parents aren't perfect, and He understands that sometimes they are unwise. But your parents are given the task of guiding and leading you until you can wisely be led and guided by God Himself. If you can't obey parents—who you can see and hear clearly—how will you learn to obey the Lord?

TO GO . . .

Read more of this letter from Paul to his friends in Colossians 3:18–25. As you go, ask God to help you have a better attitude toward obeying your parents.

> *Start a youth out on his way; even when he grows old he will not depart from it. (Proverbs 22:6)*

To succeed in any activity, you've got to learn the fundamentals. In basketball, that's dribbling, shooting, and guarding. In music, it's rhythm, harmony, and melody. Whatever the endeavor, correct fundamentals set you up for success as you develop.

The fundamentals for success in life are basically the same thing: learn how to do things the proper way when you're young so you can develop them as you get older and better. Life fundamentals include:

- great attitude
- thankfulness
- determination and endurance
- appropriate submission
- depending on, believing, and worshiping God
- hope for eternity through Jesus
- kindness and generosity

These life skills don't magically appear when you turn eighteen. You start practicing them at a young age. Your parents start you on the right path, and you develop as you get older. Start choosing God's path. Take those steps bravely.

TO GO . . .

Learn more about walking on the right way in Ecclesiastes 11:9. As you go, reflect on the list above; are you choosing to develop those skills?

All of you agree in what you say, that there be no divisions among you, and that you be united with the same understanding and the same conviction.
(1 Corinthians 1:10)

In Paul's letter to the church in Corinth, he opens with a warm greeting and a word of encouragement. Then, he gets to the heart of his letter; he's heard about fighting among the Christians at the church.

We'd like to believe that our churches would never argue. We'd also like to think that family units are always loving, kind, and agreeable. Neither are guaranteed.

But you can do something to help your family—both at home and at church. Be more loving, kinder, and less argumentative. Agree on Jesus!

When you agree on Jesus, you . . .

- put Him first.
- seek His wisdom.
- choose to love, forgive, and help.
- open your hearts and your homes to others.

TO GO . . .

Read Paul's introduction and his honest assessment of the church in 1 Corinthians 1. As you go, consider one ongoing argument in your home. Choose to forgive and love.

> *And let us watch out for one another to provoke love and good works, not neglecting to gather together, as some are in the habit of doing, but encouraging each other. (Hebrews 10:24–25)*

You've got a lot going on in your life. Between school, family, friends, sports and hobbies, and maybe even a job, you probably cherish what time you have to yourself.

But anyone who follows Jesus has been made aware that He called us not only to serve Him but also to serve others; that includes other Christians.

In today's passage you see several reasons for gathering with believers regularly:

- watching out for one another
- provoking love in each other
- provoking good works among one another
- encouraging each other

Time with other believers is beneficial for you, for them, and for the relationships you develop with one another. You need them; they need you. Jesus intended for church to work just like that.

TO GO . . .

Read about other ways you can strive toward godliness in Hebrews 10:19–23. As you go, ask God to show you how you can be more of an example or encourager in your church.

"For where two or three are gathered together in my name, I am there among them." (Matthew 18:20)

When you hear someone talking about going to "church," what comes to mind? Perhaps a big building with a steeple; maybe a converted theater or warehouse; for some it could even be a small building or a home.

But consider today's passage: when just a handful of believers are gathered to represent Him, Jesus is there. When His presence is there, you're ready to worship, praise, hear His Word, speak truth, and encourage one another in your testimony.

Your regular weekly times of congregation gathering are always important. But here are some other places you can go to "church":

- school: in class, in the hall, or in extracurricular activities
- home: at meals, time with family, or driving together
- with your friends: wherever you hang out

Don't miss an opportunity to dwell with Jesus and other believers. Experience the blessing whenever two or three are gathered in His name!

TO GO . . .

Look at other times when Jesus was among a group of believers in John 20:19 and 26. As you go, consider one place today or tomorrow you could encourage an impromptu gathering of believers.

> *Let the word of Christ dwell richly among you, in*
> *all wisdom teaching and admonishing one another*
> *through psalms, hymns, and spiritual songs,*
> *singing to God with gratitude. (Colossians 3:16)*

When you read and study and believe God's Word, it doesn't stay hidden inside you; it spreads to others!

Consider today's passage. When the Word of Christ dwells richly among us, we wisely teach and admonish (which means to give guidance and caution) through the words that come out of our mouths. Not only do you become wiser from knowing God's Word, but you also become a vessel through which others receive His truth.

Note specifically the types of speech that help spread God's Word:

- psalms
- hymns
- spiritual songs
- singing with gratitude

The truth in your heart needs an outlet; music is the perfect path. You don't have to craft a sermon or Bible study; simply let the words of truth that you sing in your church or the worship music you listen to flow out.

TO GO . . .

Read the song Moses sang to God in Deuteronomy 32. As you go, don't keep the music in your heart! Whistle, hum, or sing it.

*They devoted themselves to the apostles'
teaching, to the fellowship, to the breaking of
bread, and to prayer. (Acts 2:42)*

In today's passage, you read about some members of the earliest church: the very first people who believed in Christ and how they lived in response to faith in Jesus.

Note the things that marked their lives:

- teaching (and learning)
- fellowship (spending time together)
- breaking of bread (eating)
- prayer

Maybe these describe your time with other believers; great! If not, don't be discouraged! Spend time with other followers of Jesus not just inside your church but outside it, too.

More than Bible study or a worship time, the earliest followers of Jesus did all kinds of things together. They talked about their lives, helped one another accomplish projects, and shared meals together.

How well are you living your life with other believers? Take your relationships outside the church building. Start digging deeper into your faith, love, and serving.

TO GO . . .

Read more about the early church in Acts 2:43–47.
As you go, consider a new way you can interact with
people from your church this week.

Preach the word; be ready in season and out of season; rebuke, correct, and encourage with great patience and teaching. (2 Timothy 4:2)

Today's passage comes from a letter that Paul wrote to Timothy, a young friend of Paul's who preached at one of the earliest churches. Paul helped Timothy know how to be an effective pastor and leader at his church.

Consider these words of instruction to not just Timothy but all pastors: preach, be ready, rebuke, correct, encourage, and teach with patience.

Sounds like a hard job, don't you think? But imagine how rewarding it would be for a pastor to have men and women, boys and girls, who followed their leadership. Knowing the job description of a pastor, what are your duties as a member of the congregation?

- listen
- be teachable
- take correction
- let your preacher's words encourage

Your pastor has a responsibility to lead you; we have the responsibility to respond.

TO GO . . .

Read more of Paul's words to Timothy in 2 Timothy 4:1–8. As you go, consider showing your pastor that you appreciate him with a note, a text, or a kind word the next time you see him.

"Go make disciples of all nations, . . . teaching them to observe everything I have commanded you. And remember, I am with you always, to the end of the age." (Matthew 28:19–20)

Many Christians consider today's passage to be our primary calling as believers. These words, spoken by Jesus to His followers just before He ascended into heaven, help us focus on what it means to follow Him: making disciples.

What does it mean to make a disciple?

- make sure people hear about Jesus and see His presence in our lives
- point them to the Bible as the source of knowing and hearing God
- be led by the Spirit in obedience and helping others see what that means
- trust Jesus is near and He loves

Still, we must not miss the first word of today's passage: go. This means everywhere and anywhere. You can go: to your school, to your family, to your friend group, to your community, or to your job.

You can go to all of these places and beyond!

TO GO . . .

Read the rest of the last chapter of Matthew. As you go, ask God, "Where can I go today?" It doesn't have to be outside of your normal life.

> *Now as we have many parts in one body, and
> all the parts do not have the same function, in
> the same way we who are many are one body in
> Christ. (Romans 12:4–5)*

What if the parts of your body could talk? Would you hear your nose say, "I'm so much better than everyone else at detecting scents?" Maybe your foot would say, "We'd never get anywhere without me."

That sounds a little silly, but each part of our body has a specific purpose. We'd be pretty useless if we were made up of only eyes or fingernails or knees.

Your church is the same:

- some people lead
- some organize
- some love babies
- some make things beautiful
- some sing or play instruments
- some teach and preach
- some encourage

Churches work best when everyone identifies the role to which he or she is called. You are an integral part of the body of your church. You were made to fill a role that no one else can do like you.

TO GO . . .

Read Paul's entire thought in Romans 12:3–8. As you go, ponder some of the gifts and skills you have. Ask God to show you how best to use those in your church.

He is also the head of the body, the church; he is the beginning, the firstborn from the dead, so that he might come to have first place in everything. (Colossians 1:18)

Almost every effective group operates with a leader. Your soccer team has a captain; your student body has a president, and you answer to a boss or manager at your job.

What about your church? You may have elders, deacons, ministers, or a pastor that have authority and respect, but in all honesty your church has one leader: Jesus.

Jesus gets first place in your church because, quite honestly, He gets first place in everything:

- He was with God at creation.
- He holds everything together.
- He holds your future.
- He gives you power and guidance.
- He died for your sins and conquered death.

A healthy, God-glorifying church puts Jesus first because He is first. In order for that to happen, He must also be first in the lives and hearts of the individual members.

TO GO . . .

Read more about Jesus' first-place role in Colossians 1:15–20. As you go, analyze your own mind and heart: is there a place where Jesus is not first?

> *Now you are the body of Christ, and individual members of it. (1 Corinthians 12:27)*

A body is healthy only when everything works together. If you sit on your foot too long and the circulation is cut off, you'll quickly realize what happens when a body part isn't working as it should.

Several times throughout Scripture, the members of a church are compared to a body. And just like a body is sub-par unless everything works together, a church functions best when everyone is interacting the way they should.

That doesn't mean you need to be in constant contact with every single church member, but it does mean that you need to know . . .

- where you fit.
- where you need to interact.
- what your role is.
- who can lead you.
- who you are called to minister to.
- what you need to be learning and developing.

Don't be the paralyzed foot of your congregation; be an attached, healthy, part of your church body.

TO GO . . .

Read all of 1 Corinthians 12 to get a deeper look at a healthy church. As you go, picture yourself and other church members as a part of your church "body." Sketch what you see.

But Christ was faithful as a Son over his household. And we are that household if we hold on to our confidence and the hope in which we boast. (Hebrews 3:6)

Jesus is the head of God's household. It's a big house, containing every man, woman, and child who follows God through saving faith in Jesus. It's great to be around others who are part of that household; hopefully you're reminded that you belong each time you gather with your church for worship, prayer time, or Bible study.

Even when you're not with your church family, you can still know that you belong because of the "confidence and the hope" that goes with you even when you leave the church building.

Confidence and hope is solid and firm, an anchor for your soul. It is also . . .

- trust that Jesus is your Savior and Lord.
- thankfulness for His blessings.
- belief that you have eternity with Him.
- identity based in who God says you are: His child.

TO GO . . .

Read the first 6 verses of Hebrews 3 and learn more about your identity. As you go, put your hope and faith into words. Say one statement of faith to someone today.

They conquered him by the blood of the Lamb and by the word of their testimony; for they did not love their lives to the point of death. (Revelation 12:11)

Sometimes things seem destined to be together. Consider these powerful combinations: chocolate and strawberries, peanut butter and jelly, superheroes and sidekicks, Legolas and Gimli.

For all the good in those combos, though, there is something much more incredible: the blood of Jesus and someone talking about it. In fact, it has the power to conquer Satan.

Why?

- Jesus' blood saves us from death, gives us power over sin, and enables us to live forever with Christ.
- Our testimony reveals how salvation changed our lives, our hearts, our attitudes, and our eternities.

Jesus' blood gives you the power you need to walk in obedient faith. Your testimony strengthens not only your own life, but that of other believers around you. Faith gives you the power to face any challenge through the amazing combination of Jesus' blood and you sharing the news of salvation.

TO GO . . .

Read about this entire scene in heaven in Revelation 12:7–12. As you go, plan a time that you and some Christian friends can get together and just talk about what Jesus is doing.

Fight the good fight of the faith. Take hold of eternal life to which you were called and about which you have made a good confession in the presence of many witnesses. (1 Timothy 6:12)

Maybe you've never considered faith to be a fight; maybe you saw it as a path or a deeper understanding. But faith really is a fight.

We're not fighting unbelievers, though; our fight is with evil, itself. That seems a little overwhelming. Honestly, do you have the fighting skills necessary to fight evil?

You do! Look how Paul explained it to Timothy in today's verse: You made a good confession in the presence of many witnesses; take hold of that eternal life. When Jesus became your Lord and Savior, your testimony began: "I will follow Jesus." Your commitment to Him is forever.

So as long as you live here on earth, you'll fight the good fight. What does that mean?

- speaking the truth in love
- forgiving
- opening your heart to others
- believing God's Word and obeying it

TO GO . . .

Look at the other instructions Paul gave to this young preacher in 1 Timothy 6:11–16. As you go, take a moment to remember your own "good confession" and the people who heard it.

> *I will proclaim your name to my brothers and sisters; I will praise you in the assembly. (Psalm 22:22)*

King David, the author of today's passage, wrote many songs for worship. (We call them psalms.) Some are victorious, some are extremely sad, some are full of praise.

Psalm 22 is not a happy song. David is dealing with all kinds of trouble: physically, emotionally, and socially. He even feels abandoned by God.

About halfway through the song, though, David says some amazing words, "But you, Lord." In those three words, David's focus shifts from his own life—which was a mess—to God, who is holy and almighty.

What about you?

- Are you struggling physically, socially, emotionally, or spiritually?
- Is your focus on God or your situation?
- When was the last time your cried out to Him?

Changing your focus may not change your situation, but it may lead you to praise. Like David, we can find power and hope in looking to God and speaking His name.

TO GO . . .

Read all of Psalm 22. Keep this prayer in mind when you are going through a hard time. As you go, practice what Psalm 22:22 teaches and tell someone who God is.

I testified to both Jews and Greeks about repentance toward God and faith in our Lord Jesus. (Acts 20:21)

Paul was raised in a Jewish home. He had a Jewish education and a Jewish lifestyle. The Jews had, for many generations, followed God and obeyed His commands. Paul likely felt comfortable with the Jews. After all, he was one.

But Paul wasn't called by God to minister to the Jews only; he was also sent to the Greeks. The Greeks had a different culture, a different set of beliefs, and a different way of living. Still, he testified—or shared his story about Jesus—with both groups.

We are often more comfortable telling others about Jesus if they are similar to us if they go to the same school, live in the same part of town. or have similar background.

We are called to share Jesus with everyone. Your testimony is power-ful! God uses you to share Jesus with people who seem distant, different, or diverse. Who are the "Greeks" in your life? They need to hear about Jesus!

TO GO . . .

Read a funny story about Paul preaching to Greeks in Acts 20:7–12. As you go, ask God to point you toward some people near you who are different from you.

> *Jesus told him, "I am the way, the truth, and the life. No one comes to the Father except through me." (John 14:6)*

Believers are sometimes wary of sharing their testimony because they're not sure what to say. They fear they don't know all the right answers and might "mess it up" if someone asks them questions.

But what about this: instead of trying to answer questions with your own words, use the words already provided by the Bible. The Bible contains everything we need for a strong testimony.

For example, if someone asks who Jesus is, you can say that He is . . .

- the way, the truth, and the life (John 14:6).
- the light of the world (John 8:12).
- the good shepherd (John 10:11).
- the resurrection and the life (John 11:25).

As you come to know more of the Bible, you'll have His words in your mind and your heart. Your testimony will be bold, biblical, and strong!

TO GO . . .

Look up Jesus' other "I am" statements in John 6:35, 10:7, and 15:1. As you go, choose one of these verses to memorize. Be ready to share it when someone asks.

Do not fear what they fear or be intimidated, but in your hearts regard Christ the Lord as holy. (1 Peter 3:14–15)

People would tell you that the world is a scary place. Some examples could be:

- environmental disaster
- conflicting world powers
- dangers at home, school, and in the community
- eroding morality and ethics

These things and others, no doubt, have the potential to cause harm. However, Peter gives his friends—as well as us—distinct instruction when it comes to the things that make most people afraid: to not fear it or be intimidated by it.

Seems crazy, right? You have no power over those things; wouldn't fear be the natural reaction? Yes; if you didn't know God. But because He is holy (beyond and above us), we can believe that the things we tend to fear are in His control. If we trust Him, there's really no need to fear.

TO GO . . .

Read all of Peter's thoughts about this topic in 1 Peter 3:8–22. As you go, jot down three things you fear. Start working through that list with God.

> *"Go home to your own people, and report to them how much the Lord has done for you and how he has had mercy on you." (Mark 5:19)*

Today's passage contains the actual words of Jesus. He spoke them to a man whose life had been chaos:

- He was demon-possessed.
- He'd lived in tombs.
- He'd been shackled with chains.
- He had often hurt himself.

Jesus entered this man's life and freed him from everything that held him captive. As Jesus got in the boat to leave that community, though, the man asked to go with Jesus. Jesus, however, didn't let him; the testimony this man would share with his friends and family would point them to Christ.

Your life is a lot like this man's if you think about it. He freed you, He gave you a new purpose, and He's instructed you to tell others about Him. Jesus' power to change lives is amazing; in response, we help others see that He was the one who saved us and that His mercy is more than we could ever comprehend.

TO GO . . .

Read the entire story in Mark 5:1–20. As you go, consider all the ways Jesus changed your life. This is part of your testimony!

Just one thing: As citizens of heaven, live your life worthy of the gospel of Christ. (Philippians 1:27)

Paul wrote today's passage in a letter to a church of believers in Philippi. It's a great verse. It basically summarizes every standard, commandment, and instruction for Christians into one sentence.

This verse helps us remember:

- whose we are
- our eternal home
- how to live
- that we represent Jesus

If you know Jesus, you are a citizen—with full rights and privileges—of heaven. Only, you're not there yet. You're on a journey, and your destination is home with Christ. Today's passage seems like something Paul is saying to you as you head out the door. "Just one thing," he says, and then he tells us how to live.

As you travel this earth, your standard is the story of Jesus. His life, death, and resurrection remind you who you are and what you stand for. His mercy, love, and forgiveness are your examples. His willingness to give of Himself enables you to live sacrificially.

TO GO . . .

Read Paul's entire thought in Philippians 1:21–30.
As you go, write this verse where you'll see it and be reminded of it several times today.

Give thanks to the Lᴏʀᴅ, for he is good; his faithful love endures forever. (Psalm 107:1)

One of the most powerful aspects of your testimony is your willingness to be thankful.

It's easy to feel thankful during the good times in your life. But when was the last time you were thankful . . .

- in boring times?
- in really, really hard times?
- when people were cruel?
- when you were overwhelmed?
- when life seemed out of control?

In these situations, being thankful is rare because the bad or hard or scary stuff is so easy to see.

It's in the midst of these times that today's passage is so important. It contains two truths for which we can always be thankful: God is good and His love endures forever.

No situation changes God's identity. When you thank Him simply for being who He is, your focus shifts from earthly struggles to holy eternity; this shift of focus will strengthen your faith and give God glory.

TO GO . . .

Read all of Psalm 107, and count the number of times the word *thank* or *thanks* appears. As you go, choose to thank God for His goodness and His love right now.

And this is the testimony: God has given us eternal life, and this life is in his Son. The one who has the Son has life. The one who does not have the Son of God does not have life. (1 John 5:11–12)

Some people think of the Old Testament as the story of God and the New Testament as the story of Jesus. On the surface that would probably seem correct, but we would be wise to remember that all of the Bible—from the first words of Genesis until the last words of Revelation—point to Jesus:

- He is the only way to God.
- He is the only way to eternal life.
- His life, death, and resurrection changed everything.

God, who dwells in perfection and holiness and glory, allows us to know Him and spend eternity with Him because we believe He sent Jesus. Jesus came as a perfect sacrifice, died willingly, and defeated death in order to give us forgiveness and power.

TO GO . . .

Slowly read these powerful words from John in 1 John 5:1–13. As you go, memorize these key words about Jesus. Ask God to give you an opportunity to share them.

> *But when the kindness of God our Savior and his love*
> *for mankind appeared, he saved us—not by works of*
> *righteousness that we had done, but according to his*
> *mercy. (Titus 3:4–5)*

If you've been in church for a while, you've probably heard all kinds of phrases about salvation and getting saved. It's an important topic—maybe the most important in all of Christianity. Today's Scriptures help clarify it:

- Who saves people? God, through Jesus.
- Why did God save us? Because of His kindness.
- What saves us? Not works; God's mercy.
- Do I feel anything if I'm saved? You'll feel new and feel yourself grow.

Depending on the church, you might feel like it's up to you to be saved; maybe you feel like you need to change your life or heart before God's salvation can be offered to you.

This isn't exactly correct. Salvation is not earned; it's God's gift to you because of His kindness and mercy.

TO GO . . .

Find today's Scriptures. Circle the main idea, "he saved us . . . according to his mercy." As you go, read back through the list above. Put these statements in your own words.

*If you confess with your mouth, "Jesus is Lord,"
and believe in your heart that God raised him from
the dead, you will be saved. (Romans 10:9)*

Few things in life are truly simple. Whether it's cooking, riding a bike, or planning a trip, almost everything is more complicated than we expect.

Salvation can seem that way. It may seem like you need to do a lot of things to consider yourself saved, but Paul didn't see salvation as complicated. In fact, it only had two steps:

- With your mouth, confess Jesus is Lord. Be careful here; those aren't just words to be said. It's stating with sincerity and all truth that you give Jesus the right to rule your life.
- With your heart, believe God raised Jesus from the dead. Your heart is the center of your thoughts, emotions, and personality. If the deep-down part of you accepts the truth of the Bible, you truly believe.

Salvation is simple but profoundly significant. Can you honestly say that you are saved?

TO GO . . .

Read more about the mouth and heart in Deuteronomy 30:14 and Psalm 19:14. As you go, spend time meditating on today's passage. Let your thoughts become your prayer.

> *There is salvation in no one else, for there is no other name under heaven given to people by which we must be saved. (Acts 4:12)*

Acts 3 tells the story of Peter and John seeing a disabled man, healing him in Jesus' name, and attracting a crowd. They also drew the attention of the temple authorities, which were annoyed with the distraction.

The next day Peter and John were called in for a hearing and were asked, "By what power or in what name have you done this?" They answered with confidence: Jesus Christ of Nazareth.

Consider the parallels between that story and your own life:

- There are people all around you who need to receive love and hear about Jesus.
- Others are going to disapprove of your faith; share Jesus with them too.
- We must always be ready to speak the truth of salvation wherever we go.

Offer kindness, faith, and hope to those around you, sharing with them the only name that saves: Jesus.

TO GO . . .

Read the entire story, starting with Acts 3:1 and ending with today's passage. As you go, remind yourself that you are a representative of Jesus. Walk in that identity.

"No one can come to me unless the Father who sent me draws him, and I will raise him up on the last day." (John 6:44)

Picture a dog owner holding up a dog's favorite toy and whistling; the owner has drawn the dog to himself, and the dog comes running.

Similarly, God draws us to Himself with His love.

Has the Father ever drawn you to Himself? It might seem like this:

- The words of Scripture come to life in a way you've never known.
- Worship music draws you to focus on God and who He is.
- A pastor's sermon or a teacher's lesson seems to be just for you.
- Everything in your life seems to be pointing you to God.

Salvation is following Jesus as Lord, but don't miss this truth: if there is anything inside you that is pulling you to say yes to Jesus, that's God the Father. He loves you, He calls you, He pulls you to Himself.

TO GO . . .

Read today's passage in context in John 6:22–59. As you go, thank God for drawing you closer to Him. Thank Him for loving you enough to make you His own.

> *The salvation of the righteous is from the LORD,*
> *their refuge in a time of distress. The LORD helps*
> *and delivers them. (Psalm 37:39–40)*

Hopefully you know what to do when dangerous weather is heading your way. Whether it's a tornado, hurricane, or flood, you should know where to seek refuge. A refuge is a safe place to go in times of trouble. For a person who has salvation, God is a refuge from all kinds of storms we face in life.

God is your refuge. What does that mean?

- He handles our fears and anxieties.
- He has a plan for us.
- He understands who we are and our struggles.
- He is with us and plans for our salvation.

Salvation is more than simply going to heaven when you die; it means that God is your refuge now and forever.

TO GO . . .

Read more about God being a refuge in Psalm 18:2 and 62:7. As you go, sketch a picture of God as your refuge. Remind yourself of that image when you are in a stormy season in life.

Jesus answered, "Truly I tell you, unless someone is born of water and the Spirit, he cannot enter the kingdom of God." (John 3:5)

Today's passage may seem a little confusing; it was to Nicodemus, a ruler of the Jews, the man listening to Jesus when He spoke the words.

Nicodemus hadn't asked how to be saved, and yet Jesus told him anyway. Why? Well, deep down, it was the answer to the question he most needed to ask.

It's also the most important question you can know the answer to and tell others: How can I be saved?

- Be born of water, which simply means that you are born as a human.
- Be born of the Spirit, meaning that the Holy Spirit lives inside you. This comes only through the saving faith in Jesus.

The kingdom of God is not an earthly kingdom; it's a spiritual kingdom. Wherever God is king, that is the kingdom of God. We enter that kingdom when the Spirit lives in us.

TO GO . . .

Read more about the Spirit's presence at salvation in 2 Corinthians 1:22. As you go, consider how the Holy Spirit lives and works in your life. Does the Spirit confirm your citizenship in the kingdom of God?

167 *SALVATION*

For the wages of sin is death, but the gift of God is eternal life in Christ Jesus our Lord. (Romans 6:23)

If you have a part-time job, you know that it takes quite a few hours to make $50. On the other hand, you might have a generous parent or grandparent who gives you $50 for your birthday.

What's the difference between earning something and it being given as a gift?

Today's passage talks about earning wages and being given a gift, but not money; it's about the difference of sin and eternal life.

- The wages of sin is death. Any person who has ever sinned— that's everyone—has earned death.
- Eternal life is a gift. There's no way to earn it; God gives it to you through Jesus.

Every part of your body—from your mind to your heart to your hands and feet—was pointed to sin at birth. God's gift allows us to break away from that slavery to sin and receive the gift of eternity with Him!

TO GO . . .

Read Paul's entire thought about sin, slavery, and more in Romans 6:15–23. As you go, thank God that your salvation is not earned; praise Him for His amazing gift!

*Guide me in your truth and teach me, for you are
the God of my salvation; I wait for you all day long.
(Psalm 25:5)*

Salvation is a gift from God; we receive it by grace when we accept Jesus
as our Lord.

However, salvation is not meant to be a one-time event, checking
the box that we're going to heaven. Salvation is an essential Step 1,
but there's so much more! After salvation, we learn how to develop that
salvation into a life that follows the Lord:

- We grow in maturity, wisdom, and faith.
- We obey and believe God's Word.
- We choose to love, forgive, and serve.
- Our worship, praise, and thankfulness grow deeper and more
  genuine.

Today's passage reveals the key to our ever-growing salvation: waiting for God to guide us. Through His Word, we seek to know Him and find
His guidance through truth. As we wait, we discover more of who He is
and how He speaks to us.

TO GO . . .

Read more about the process of salvation and waiting
in Isaiah 25:9 and 33:2. As you go, consider one area
in which you need guidance. Commit to wait on God to
lead you.

If we confess our sins, he is faithful and righteous to forgive us our sins and to cleanse us from all unrighteousness. (1 John 1:9)

Confession isn't fun, but it's so necessary! It's a cleansing part of walking with Jesus. If we go for a period of time without confession, we've done the spiritual equivalent of skipping showers. The dirt and grime of sin eventually get caked on; confession helps us see our own sin.

The word for confess is actually a combination of two Greek words:

- *homou,* which means "together" or "the same"
- *logos*, which means "word"

When we confess, we are saying the same words about ourselves that God would say about us. Confession is agreeing with God. Basically, that means we look at God's Word and say, "Lord, I need you. You are almighty. You love me and I am your child." With those words serving as the foundation, we agree with God about our sin and believe that He forgives us and cleanses us!

TO GO . . .

Look at another verse about confession in 1 John 4:15. As you go, ask God to bring to mind some areas in your life that need confession. Agree with God!

He himself bore our sins in his body on the tree; so that, having died to sins, we might live for righteousness. By his wounds you have been healed. (1 Peter 2:24)

Sin kills. That sounds harsh, but it's the truth. Sin is powerful, enslaving, and brings forth death; you're not strong enough to defeat sin.

But Jesus is. Because He was fully God and fully man, Jesus' death . . .

- removed the power of sin.
- gave us the victory over sin.
- healed us of sin's effects.
- provided the power to live in victory over sin.

When Jesus died, He carried our sins with Him to the cross. We can't understand completely how Jesus' sacrifice paid for our sins. Today's passage, however, gives us assurance that we no longer need to worry about the death that sin brings or the power it has over us; Jesus' death gives us victory over sin and death.

Have you accepted Jesus' amazing gift? Are you walking in freedom from your sin?

TO GO . . .

Read more about Jesus' sacrifice for you in 1 Peter 2:21–25. As you go, picture Jesus suffering for you. Thank Him, praise Him, and give your life to Him.

Lord, who is like you among the gods? Who is like you, glorious in holiness, revered with praises, performing wonders? (Exodus 15:11)

Today's passage is found in a worship song led by Moses after he and the children of Israel had walked away from slavery in Egypt and crossed the God-parted Red Sea.

In that impromptu praise gathering, they were focused on the holiness of God. The concept of holiness is complex, but at its root, it contains the idea of being separate:

- God is far away from all other "gods."
- God's power and strength are superior.
- God's miracles blow away any other feat.
- God's love for us is higher and more powerful than any other love.

When we consider God—who He is and what He does—we can't help but be astounded at how amazing He is. God's holiness—His separateness—are what make Him worthy of our praise. The Israelites praised the holiness of God; we should too. Speak or write or sing about His holiness today.

TO GO . . .

Read the words of Moses' entire song in Exodus 15:1–18. As you go, make a mental list of how God is separate from everything and everyone else.

Then he consulted with the people and appointed some to sing for the Lord and some to praise the splendor of his holiness. (2 Chronicles 20:21)

Today's passage contains part of the story of Jehoshaphat, king of Judah. He had just gotten news that many of his enemies had joined forces and were headed towards them to fight. Jehoshaphat declared a fast and led His people in prayer to God for help. God responded, telling them to not be afraid; He would fight, not them.

On the day of the attack, Jehoshaphat's army marched out in formation, led by worshipers. On the way to battle, they sang, "Give thanks to the Lord, for his faithful love endures forever."

What gave the Israelites the idea to sing praise?

- They had heard from the Lord and believed He would give them victory.
- They trusted in His holiness and believed He would defeat their enemy.
- They wanted to depend on God and not themselves for victory.

God was faithful; He set an ambush against their enemies and completely defeated them.

TO GO . . .

Read about God's mighty victory in 2 Chronicles 20:1–30. As you go, choose to worship as you head toward difficult situations. Focus on God's holiness.

173 HOLINESS

> *Ascribe to the L ORD, you heavenly beings, ascribe to the L ORD glory and strength. Ascribe to the L ORD the glory due his name; worship the L ORD in the splendor of his holiness. (Psalm 29:1–2)*

Ascribe may not be a word you regularly use. It can mean "give" or "assign," with the idea of connecting a person with a quality. When you mention someone's talent or skills, you're ascribing honor to them for it.

In today's passage, David is addressing not only the congregation in worship but also the mightiest of all: heavenly beings. He is commanding them to . . .

- acknowledge God's glory and strength.
- assign glory to God's name and identity.
- lift up God, recognizing His beautiful holiness.

When we worship and praise God, we are joining with the angels and the heavenly beings who are constantly ascribing glory and honor to God's holiness. Acknowledging God's glory and strength enables us to focus on Him as He truly is: supremely holy.

TO GO . . .

Read all of Psalm 29. Picture King David and the Israelite worshipers singing and praising. As you go, join David and the Israelite worshipers in ascribing glory to God! Tell Him how holy He is!

"I will display my greatness and holiness, and will reveal myself in the sight of many nations. Then they will know that I am the Lᴏʀᴅ." (Ezekiel 38:23)

What makes God, well, God?

You know what makes a snake a snake: slithery, scaly, flicking tongue. You know what makes a bee a bee: makes honey, stinger, gathers pollen. You even know what makes your mom your mom: the characteristics that set her apart from everyone else.

Same with God: His holiness—the things that only He can do and only He does—are what make Him God.

Consider a few descriptions of the holiness of God:

- He created and maintains all things.
- He has power over everything He created.
- He has always existed, and He always will.
- He bestows His favor, blessing, and love out of mercy.

God reveals Himself through His holiness. Can you see it? Even better, are you pointing Him out to others? Are you a vessel through which others can see the holiness of God?

TO GO . . .

Learn more about God revealing His holiness in Nehemiah 9:14, Luke 10:21, and Revelation 15:4. As you go, look for the things that point you to God. Praise Him when you see them.

> *He has given us the privilege, since we have been rescued from the hand of our enemies, to serve him without fear in holiness and righteousness in his presence all our days. (Luke 1:73–75)*

Today's passage comes from a prophecy made by Zechariah, the father of John the Baptist. In it, Zechariah finds many reasons to praise God:

- He redeemed His people.
- He provided salvation.
- He gave mercy.
- He remembered His covenant.
- He rescued from enemies.

Because of these things, we—who for thousands of years have believed in God's salvation—have the privilege to serve Him without fear, in holiness and righteousness. If you fear or dread serving God, you probably don't have a clear vision of who He is. Get to know Him better through reading His Word; choose to believe He is who He says He is and that He can do what He says He can do. Because of His all-surpassing power, we can serve Him confidently, knowing that He is in control.

TO GO . . .

Read Zechariah's entire prophecy in Luke 1:67–79. As you go, start your own list of reasons to praise God. Start with the items in Zechariah's prophecy.

So then, dear friends, since we have these
promises, let us cleanse ourselves from every
impurity of the flesh and spirit, bringing holiness to
completion in the fear of God. (2 Corinthians 7:1)

At the end of 2 Corinthians 6, Paul combined several Old Testament passages into one beautiful description about God. Paul reports that God . . .

- dwells with us.
- is our God and we are His people.
- calls us to be separate and clean.
- welcomes us.
- is our Father.

This list is far from thorough; however, it helps us stare into the truth of who God is.

Today's passage says, "So then." This comes immediately after this list. Because of who God is, we are to cleanse ourselves—body and spirit—to complete holiness.

That's a powerful statement: God's holiness is made complete when we, like Him, are also holy. As we know and believe who God is, we choose to be cleansed and different from the world so that we point people to God.

TO GO . . .

Read Paul's description of God and us in 2 Corinthians 6:16–18. As you go, analyze your daily life: where do you conform? Where are you holy?

> *May he make your hearts blameless in holiness*
> *before our God and Father at the coming*
> *of our Lord Jesus with all his saints. Amen.*
> *(1 Thessalonians 3:13)*

The holiness of God has a purpose. Not only does it enable us to be holy and follow Him, but according to today's passage, it also makes our hearts blameless.

You know the condition of your heart; it's nowhere near perfect. Blameless, however, doesn't mean perfect; its meaning is closer to "free from fault" or "without defect." Think of it like a delicious banana—yellow and beautiful—compared to an over ripened banana—brownish and mushy.

As we choose holiness, God makes our hearts blameless. A blameless heart is healthy, full, and overflowing. What does that look like in real life?

- We truly love others.
- We willingly forgive and serve.
- We seek God's glory in all we do.
- We open our lives to those who need Jesus.

A blameless heart can be yours. Offer it to Jesus in holiness.

TO GO . . .

Learn more about being blameless in Philippians 2:15 and Luke 1:6. As you go, sketch a picture of your heart as it is now. How healthy is it? Where is it in need of renewal?

*Pursue peace with everyone, and holiness—
without it no one will see the Lord. (Hebrews
12:14)*

Today's passage is short and simple—on the surface, at least. You could probably memorize it in five minutes. Believing it, though, is a different story. Actually doing it is even harder.

Let's break it down into these two simple commands:

- pursue peace with everyone
- pursue holiness

The concept of pursuing is no passive verb; it contains the idea of running swiftly in order to catch the thing you're chasing. In the world of sports, it's the person you're supposed to be guarding in basketball: you keep your eyes on the player, stick with him, and don't let him go.

With that same intensity and tenacity, we pursue peace. Not just your friends or the family members you enjoy but with everyone. On top of that, we pursue holiness—being set apart for God's use.

Pursuing peace and holiness isn't simple, but it's a mature way to live and our command and goal.

TO GO . . .

Read what else we are to pursue in Romans 14:19 and 1 Corinthians 14:1. As you go, picture yourself running after peace and holiness. What action does that prompt you to take?

> *"For I am the LORD, who brought you up from the land of Egypt to be your God, so you must be holy because I am holy." (Leviticus 11:45)*

There's a good chance you've never read the book of Leviticus with excitement. It can seem tedious, filled with specific standards and measurements and details for how the Israelites were to live and worship.

Today's passage, however, explains why God has authority:

- He is Yahweh, the I am.
- He brought the Israelites out of slavery.
- He is holy—separate and above everything else.

God's plan was never to have a democracy. He has full authority because His knowledge, His power, and His plan are so far and above anything we could ever fathom.

What, then, does He call us to do? Be holy, like He is holy. That doesn't mean to be holy in the way that God is holy: all-powerful, all-knowing, and everywhere. Instead, we're commanded to be different from the world in order to point others to Him.

TO GO . . .

Glance through Leviticus and choose a chapter to read. As you go, whisper, "God is holy; I am holy," to yourself several times. See how this changes your day.

And one called to another: "Holy, holy, holy is the
Lord of Armies; his glory fills the whole earth."
(Isaiah 6:3)

What's the most opulent, fancy, exquisite sight you've ever seen? Maybe it was a mansion, a castle, or a governmental building? Even if you've seen the Taj Mahal or the Burj Khalifa, they don't compare with what Isaiah saw.

Isaiah, a prophet of God, was able to glimpse into the throne room of heaven. He saw . . .

- God on His throne.
- God's robe filling the temple.
- heavenly beings flying all around, singing.

The heavenly beings, identified as seraphim, had six wings. Their voices were so powerful that they shook the foundations of the doorways when they called to one another. Maybe they were exceedingly loud; or perhaps it was what they said that had power.

You'll find their words in today's passage: God is holy, He is Lord of everything, and His glory fills the earth. This is the core identity of God, and the one that has the most power in your life, as well.

TO GO . . .

Read the whole scene in detail in Isaiah 6:1–8. As you go, allow your mind to picture this scene for just a few minutes. Join the seraphim in praising God's holiness.

181 FREEDOM

> *For freedom, Christ set us free. Stand firm then and don't submit again to a yoke of slavery.*
> *(Galatians 5:1)*

Freedom is one of the most sought-after conditions in humanity. The opposite of freedom is captivity; those that are enslaved and entrapped suffer in so many ways.

Consider what happens to people who are not free:

- They lose their ability to choose.
- Their movements and actions are restricted.
- Their rights to act, speak, or think are restrained.

As terrible and oppressive as captivity is for people all around the world, every single person alive faces the struggle of captivity to sin. A person can live in the most liberated nation in the world and still find themselves emotionally, spiritually, and mentally enslaved to sin. But for those whose Savior is Jesus, we are no longer bound to that sin; He sets us free.

We walk in freedom from sin when we choose to believe and obey Christ. Standing firm means identifying temptation and choosing to rely on Christ's power over sin.

TO GO . . .

Read more about being a slave to sin in John 8:34. As you go, ponder your own life: Has sin enslaved you? How?

Our fathers trusted in you; they trusted, and you rescued them. They cried to you and were set free; they trusted in you and were not disgraced. (Psalm 22:4–5)

There is a recurring cycle of sin in the Old Testament:

- God's people sin in idolatry.
- God allows their enemies to enslave them.
- God's people cry out; He hears them.
- God frees His people, and they obey Him.
- Repeat.

In today's passage, David is remembering the faithfulness of God: He rescued and set free the people who cried out to Him. King David, like all Israelites, could trace his lineage back to Abraham; he would have known the faithfulness of God to His chosen people.

Just as God loved, heard, and rescued His people in the Old Testament, He does the same for His children today. He doesn't simply want to get you out of your mess, though; He wants to set you free from sin. And when you are free, your story becomes one of hope and points others to salvation.

TO GO . . .

Read more about David being set free in Psalm 144. As you go, take a moment to recall your own life: when was the last time you called out to God?

Now the Lord is the Spirit, and where the Spirit of the Lord is, there is freedom. (2 Corinthians 3:17)

You might know quite a bit about God, already. You may know many of the stories and identities of Jesus. But how much do you know about the Spirit?

In today's passage, we see that Jesus—the Lord—is the Spirit. Just as the Father and the Son are one in their purpose and their plan, so is Jesus and the Spirit; Jesus dwells inside you through the Spirit. When the Spirit is inside you, there is freedom . . .

- to worship God with our whole mind, heart, and personality.
- to say no to sin.
- to walk in full faith of God, believing His Word.
- to be the person God created you to be.

Obedience is certainly part of following Jesus; those who have Jesus as Lord give Him authority in their lives. Christianity, however, is not about following rules just to be obedient. When we follow Christ, we find the freedom that comes from His leadership in our lives.

TO GO . . .

Learn more about the Spirit in John 16:12–15. As you go, ask God to show you the freedom that comes from the Spirit.

Then Jesus said to the Jews who had believed him, "If you continue in my word, you really are my disciples. You will know the truth, and the truth will set you free." (John 8:31–32)

What does it mean to be a disciple of Jesus? The word *disciple* has a root meaning of "learner," so, anyone who sets out to *learn* what it means to live like Jesus is, in fact, His disciple.

In today's passage, Jesus Himself describes what it means to be a disciple: we must continue in His Word. But what does that mean?

- We read, study, meditate on, and memorize the Bible.
- We apply it to our lives and share its truth with others.
- We are never satisfied with our knowledge of Scripture; we believe it is how God speaks to us, so we dig deeper and deeper.

Continuing in the Bible leads to the truth of who God is and who you are. His Word, made alive in the Holy Spirit, leads to freedom.

TO GO . . .

Read more about truth and freedom in John 8:30–47. As you go, assess your time and attention to the Word of God: are you continuing in it?

> *But now, since you have been set free from sin and have become enslaved to God, you have your fruit, which results in sanctification—and the outcome is eternal life! (Romans 6:22)*

Today's passage seems to be bad news on the surface: You are a slave. That seems like a terrible thing; no one would ever choose slavery. However, there is a spiritual principle that is true regardless of our opinion about it: We are either a slave to sin or we are a slave to Christ.

Does that seem harsh? Don't you wish you could be a slave to nothing? Sorry; the only way to get out of slavery to sin is through Jesus, and He requires us to deny ourselves, take up our crosses, and follow Him (Luke 9:23).

Don't fret, though: being a slave of God has amazing benefits:

- access to His wisdom, power, and love
- sanctification—being made more and more holy
- fruitful lives, revealing our identity with Him
- eternal life

TO GO . . .

Read Romans 6:15–23 slowly. Circle the words *sin* and *slave* every time they appear. As you go, start a list in your journal and title it, "Benefits of Being a Slave of God." Start with today's bulleted list.

I will walk freely in an open place because I study your precepts. (Psalm 119:45)

Today's passage comes from the longest chapter in the Bible: 176 verses! Almost all of them say something like this:

- "I love the Word of God."
- "God's Word is perfect."
- "All I need is God's Word."

Verse 45 follows the standard set for this beautiful psalm. The psalmist is singing about the freedom that comes from studying God's precepts—His commandments, statutes, and standards.

Most people who know about God but don't have a relationship with God think that sounds terrible. They don't want to obey an ancient set of rules. However, people who believe God's love for them, and believe His Word speaks the truth of His love, understand the concept of true freedom.

You can only walk in freedom when you know and believe God through His Word. It protects you, guides you, shows you who God is, reveals truth, and opens your mind to the Spirit.

TO GO . . .

Try to read all of Psalm 119. I promise it's worth it! As you go, make a quick mental list of good reasons to study the Bible.

For you were called to be free, brothers and sisters; only don't use this freedom as an opportunity for the flesh, but serve one another through love. (Galatians 5:13)

Sometimes people who have been set free forget what used to keep them captive, and sin is the greatest captor in all of history. When Jesus comes into a life, He frees a person from sin. Now, instead of answering to sin in their lives, they find the freedom of living in Christ.

But sin never stops calling; it whispers things like:

- "It's not a big deal."
- "No one will know."
- "You deserve it."
- "It's okay; you do almost everything right."

These are lies. Jesus freed you from sin the moment you believed in Him; don't be fooled again. Any time you choose sin over Jesus, you're living for yourself and not living for Him.

The antidote to sin's lies? According to today's passage, one way to overcome sin is in serving others. Hand out water, help a child, teach truth, and go wherever you have the opportunity in Jesus' name.

TO GO . . .

Continue reading Paul's thought in Galatians 5:13–25. As you go, be aware of the lies of sin. Walk in the freedom to love, serve, and help others.

Therefore, there is now no condemnation for those in Christ Jesus, because the law of the Spirit of life in Christ Jesus has set you free from the law of sin and death. (Romans 8:1–2)

The idea of *condemnation* found in today's passage is a judicial term: the declaration that one is guilty.

But I am guilty, many believers think. Consider these truths, though:

- God loves you regardless of your past or your sinful nature.
- In Jesus, you are forgiven of every sin.
- You no longer owe a debt for your sin.
- The death of Jesus paid the debt for every sin, past and future.

So, though you may sin, you are not guilty. Though you choose against God, He does not hold you under the condemnation of your sin. The freedom He gives will strengthen you to live a holy life.

A guilty verdict of sin is punishable by death, but you are not guilty! You are washed clean by the blood of Jesus.

TO GO . . .

Read more about not being condemned in John 3:17 and Romans 5:18. As you go, picture the words "Not guilty" above your head. How does it feel to walk in freedom?

> *I called to the LORD in distress; the LORD answered*
> *me and put me in a spacious place. (Psalm 118:5)*

What was the longest time you ever spent in a car? After several hours, your muscles ache, everyone gets on your nerves, you can't sleep, and all you want is to get out. When you finally stop, everyone in the car is excited to move around in freedom.

That's the same feeling we get when we cry out to the Lord and He answers us: He puts us in a spacious place. God's spacious place is a picture of freedom where . . .

- you have room to grow and expand.
- your mind, soul, and spirit feel free.
- you can express your emotions and think clearly.

As life closes in around you, the strain of stress, worry, and hopelessness constrict you. But you don't have to stay there; call out to the Lord, and He will answer you. The spacious place God gives is not physical; He opens our hearts to dwell in it spiritually.

TO GO . . .

Read more about a spacious place in 2 Samuel 22:20 and Psalm 18:19. As you go, speak out loud to God the things that are restricting or constraining you.

Speak and act as those who are to be judged
the law of freedom. (James 2:12)

Today's verse points to the real-life, every day, can-you-h
instruction: Speaking and acting in freedom.

You see, you're free. Jesus said so when you said yes
tion to salvation. Freedom is one of the many benefits of f
wholeheartedly:

- You're free to follow Jesus wherever He leads
- You're free to serve others without fear.
- You're free to love everyone—seriously, e'
- You're free to be grateful, generous, and ç

When we live in freedom, we understand the b
our hearts and want others to know it, too. We wan
dom that Jesus gives as we interact with others, wh
easy or hard to love.

So, we speak and act in freedom: We stay away fi
biting, hateful, rude, petty, or spiteful. We avoid acts th
ceived as unkind, uncaring, unloving, or selfish. Is you
through your words and actions?

TO GO . . .

Read the rest of James' thought in James 2:
go, consider a time today when you'll need t
act in freedom. Make plans to do it.

...n't worry about anything, but in everything,
...ough prayer and petition with thanksgiving,
...ent your requests to God. (Philippians 4:6)

...be in a stressful situation, like a test you're not ready for
...ber struggling with health issues, and have someone tell
...worry about it." You probably want to say, "Yeah, okay!
...worry about things that we can't control or handle.

...'t worry about it." is exactly what Paul told the church
...s passage. He didn't expect them to simply ignore or
...e stress; he prescribed the solution for it:

...thing

...everything

...od

...orrying is found in the power and presence of God
...an handle your stresses. God has a plan to not
...that situation but to make you victorious and bring
...hand those requests to God, you can believe He has

...full thought in Philippians 4:4–7. As you
...aul's instructions literally: write down your
...d pray over them.

Humble yourselves, therefore, under the mighty hand of God, so that he may exalt you at the proper time, casting all your cares on him, because he cares about you. (1 Peter 5:6–7)

You've been told that it's good to be strong, to stand up for yourself, to set your sights high.

In some areas, like school, relationships, or sports, this can be true. But in the spiritual realm, the best advice is to do just the opposite: humble yourself.

Humbling oneself is willingly making oneself lower. How in the world is this a healthy position for a Christ follower?

- You recognize your own shortcomings.
- You admit your faults and weakness.
- You give God control and authority.
- You agree that He is God and you are not.

God's hand is mighty; He can handle the things that bring you down. Give Him control and authority over your life. When the time is right—according to His perfect plan—He will give you the strength to handle whatever He has placed in your life.

TO GO . . .

Read all of 1 Peter 5, which is the end of his letter. As you go, plan a time today to literally get low: bow, kneel, or sit. Quote this verse aloud.

> *"But seek first the kingdom of God and his righteousness, and all these things will be provided for you." (Matthew 6:33)*

Today's passage comes from the mouth of Jesus, in the midst of one of His most famous sermons. In the verses preceding it, He instructed His followers:

- Don't worry about your life.
- Don't worry about what you eat or drink.
- Don't worry about what you wear.
- Your Father knows what you need.

Instead, He told them to seek the kingdom of God. Take the mental energy, the emotions, the time, and the focus you would have spent on these everyday items and focus instead on God's plan.

Clothing and food are a cause for worry for some people around the world because of poverty. For some, clothing and food are status symbols, communicating wealth. Most people in the world worry about these things for one reason or another, but we glorify God when we choose to look to Him instead.

TO GO . . .

Read this entire section of the Sermon on the Mount in Matthew 6:25–34. As you go, stop and analyze your heart: are you worried about those things? How can you trust Jesus and obey this command?

Anxiety in a person's heart weighs it down, but a good word cheers it up. (Proverbs 12:25)

Dealing with anxiety is hard. As today's passage states, our anxiety weighs our heart down. It makes us feel burdened and we struggle to find joy.

But today's passage also tells us how we can help a friend who is weighed down with anxiety: by speaking a good word to them. What constitutes a good word? The Hebrew word for *good* has many meanings:

- kind, upright, and merciful
- fair or beautiful
- pleasant, agreeable, or happy
- distinguished, great, or excellent
- cheerful or merry

God used the word when He created everything and declared it "good" in Genesis 1; it's the same word used to describe God in Psalm 34:8.

So when a friend is anxious, make it your goal to speak a good word: one that is honest, pleasant, excellent, and points them to God. Good words encourage, uplift and speak truth to a situation.

TO GO . . .

Find a deeper meaning of this word in Psalm 34:14 and Deuteronomy 6:18. As you go, consider one or two good words you can speak to a friend today.

> *"Come to me, all of you who are weary and burdened, and I will give you rest." (Matthew 11:28)*

Have you ever found yourself weary or burdened? Have you ever felt overwhelmed by a situation or many situations? Are you tired all the time? Do you feel helpless or hopeless?

In today's passage, Jesus has invited you to come to Him. What does that mean?

- spend time alone with Him, thinking or talking about your struggles prayerfully
- invite Him to carry your burdens
- trust Him for the solution to the problem
- find wisdom and encouragement in His Word

The picture here is of you carrying a backpack that is way too heavy; it weighs you down. Jesus is offering to carry it for you and give you rest from the struggle and burden. Whatever it is that you're carrying, He is strong enough to handle it. He is wise enough to know what to do. He is loving enough to do what is best.

TO GO . . .

See what Jeremiah 6:16 teaches about another place to find rest. As you go, plan a time to sit in silence for five minutes today and give your burdens to Jesus.

"Peace I leave with you. My peace I give to you. I do not give to you as the world gives. Don't let your heart be troubled or fearful." (John 14:27)

Today's passage comes from Jesus' last night with His disciples. It was Passover; He had enjoyed a meal with them and had just revealed to them that He was going to God. He had promised them He was going to prepare a place for them and that the Holy Spirit would comfort them.

They, of course, had fears, concerns, and questions. The disciples often remind us of ourselves: we want to follow Jesus, but we struggle to honestly believe Him. Regardless of the concerns, Jesus gave His disciples—and He gives to us—the promise of peace:

- He is the Prince of peace, and He leaves His peace with us.
- His peace is not like the peace of the world.
- His peace enables us to have a heart that is not troubled or fearful.

TO GO . . .

Read John 14:27–31 and ask Jesus to help you believe His promise of peace. As you go, give your stress to Jesus. Ask for His peace to fill you.

> *Cast your burden on the Lord, and he will sustain you; he will never allow the righteous to be shaken. (Psalm 55:22)*

Sometimes, we're going through life and everything seems to be just fine. Then, out of nowhere, something comes along that shakes us: a broken relationship, a sickness or disease, a natural disaster, or maybe even a death.

In today's passage, we are promised that God will never allow the righteous to be shaken. Righteous people are forgiven because of Jesus' death and resurrection. If you are a follower of Jesus, you are righteous.

Does that mean those who love and follow God are never going to experience those tragedies? No, but it does mean that He helps us to bear them. How?

- He carries our burdens. When we admit that our situations are too much for us, He is able and willing to carry the struggle and stress of it.

- He sustains us: God gives us the ability to keep going and face our struggles.

TO GO . . .

Read more about not being shaken in Psalm 17:5, 21:7, and 46:2. As you go, reflect on the times your world has been shaken. How did God sustain you?

"Do not fear, for I am with you; do not be afraid, for I am your God. I will strengthen you; I will help you; I will hold on to you with my righteous right hand." (Isaiah 41:10)

When you were a child, you probably feared scary movies, thunder, bad dreams, or mean dogs. As a teenager, you fear different things. Fearful things don't go away just because we get older; there are plenty of things that adults fear, as well.

So how do we obey God's commands of "do not fear" and "do not be afraid" in today's passage? We put our focus on God.

- He is with you.
- He is your God.
- He will strengthen you.
- He will hold on to you with His righteous right hand.

God doesn't instruct us to not fear and then send us off on our own! The reason we can face our world without fear is because of Him! He is with us. He is almighty. He has us. In order to obey, then, we choose to keep our focus on Him.

TO GO . . .

Read more of these encouraging words in Isaiah 41:8–13. As you go, set your thoughts on God through His Word, prayer, and worship.

> *"Haven't I commanded you: be strong and courageous? Do not be afraid or discouraged, for the LORD your God is with you wherever you go." (Joshua 1:9)*

God raised up Moses, a mighty warrior, to lead the people out of slavery in Egypt. He was a leader like few others: brave, bold, focused. Like a successful coach who retires, no one wants to follow in those shoes. Nevertheless, Joshua got the job.

Today's passage contains the words God spoke to Joshua. Joshua knew what it meant to lead the Israelites: they were hard-headed and hard-hearted, prone to rebel and grumble. On top of that, Joshua's job was to lead them into battle and take over the Promised Land. Few tasks likely seemed more daunting than the one he was about to face.

In this one chapter, God uses the phrase "strong and courageous" four times. Why? Because:

- Joshua needed to be reminded.
- Joshua felt weak and fearful.
- God was with him; he could be strong and courageous.

TO GO . . .

Read Joshua 1. Hear God speaking these words to you. As you go, consider where you find yourself weak and fearful. Ask God to help you be strong and courageous.

When I am afraid, I will trust in you. In God, whose word I praise, in God I trust; I will not be afraid. (Psalm 56:3–4)

There are certain things in life that inspire us to take immediate action:

- When we're cold, we put on a coat.
- When we're sad, we listen to music or watch a funny video.
- When we're hungry, we grab something to eat.

These come naturally, but there are times when we need to train our heart and mind to respond to life in a particular way. Today's passage is one of them: when you feel afraid, trust in God.

For most of us, the first response to fear is panic or dread. David's words today remind us that our first instinct should be to trust God.

How do we trust in God? Do what David instructed: dig into His Word and praise Him. You'll be amazed at the power these two actions have over your fear.

TO GO . . .

Read all of Psalm 56. Ask God to help you apply these words to your own life. As you go, memorize half or all of this verse. Repeat it several times—silently or aloud—throughout the day.